Publication Number 3 in the "On Target"
Series of Outdoor Sports Publications
from Glenn Helgeland's
TARGET COMMUNICATIONS

First Edition
First Printing 8/83
Second Printing 4/85
Third Printing 8/86

On Target for

TAKING TROPHY WHITETAILS

by Bob Fratzke
with Glenn Helgeland

Library of Congress Number: 83-050905

TARGET COMMUNICATIONS CORPORATION
7626 W. Donges Bay Rd.
Mequon, WI 53092

ISBN: 0913305022

i

Note from Bob Fratzke:

I'm grateful Glenn Helgeland wrote this book with me and published it. He knows what whitetail hunting is all about, and he can put it on paper in a way you'll understand and enjoy. We found several times when we were preparing the book that I'd start a statement and he would finish it, or he would start one and I'd finish it. In addition, some of the basic items have become such second-nature to me that they could have been overlooked in our preparation of this book, but his editing and writing experience helped solve that problem.

Some items or parts of items in the book are purposely repetitive. It's easy to miss important points if they're mentioned only once, so a second mention usually helps the material catch on.

Just remember, in your whitetail hunting, there is never "always" and there is never "never" in regard to whitetail behavior. The whitetail deer will always be a whitetail deer ... frustrating at times, fascinating all the time. It's a wonderful animal.

We hope our love for and respect of this animal show throughout the book. That's what it deserves.

Bob Fratzke

Publisher's Note:

If you use the things Bob has to say about taking trophy whitetails, you'll get a lot of good ideas — and probably some good deer. Something as apparently complex as whitetail hunting takes clear thinking to break it down to the simple elements of food, cover, movement, reproduction — and then put those elements back together in a manner which will have you well on the road toward taking trophy whitetails.

I've hunted with Bob a lot, yet every time we hunt together, every time we talk about hunting, I pick up something useful. That makes it even more fun.

Glenn Helgeland, President
Target Communications Corporation
Mequon, Wisconsin

CONTENTS

• *The whitetail buck . . . elusive, fascinating, Photo by Mark LaBarbera.*

Chapter 1
Define Your Hunting Goals

The whitetail deer is a tremendous game animal. It is a challenge, a supreme challenge. Lots of hunters would like to believe it is a mysterious animal. It's not mysterious, there just are plenty of things we haven't learned about it yet. Putting it into the mystery category does only one thing — takes the fault off our shoulders, mentally, when we don't get a deer. That makes us feel better, but it is the wrong conclusion.

The whitetail comes the closest among North American big game to being "everyman's" quarry. It is the most widespread species. It can — and does — live comfortably right under our noses, but we seldom see it. I know that if we ever got a chance to see all the deer there are in some areas, we'd be astonished, and if we could see all the good bucks there are everywhere, we'd be equally astonished.

Not only is the whitetail the closest to being every bowhunter's main huntable animal, **it also is the number one trophy, in my book.** If you have the money, are able to travel, get the right guide/outfitter, you can take any kind of trophy animal, *excluding trophy whitetails*. With whitetails, you have to pretty well do it yourself. Just try to tally the number of hours all U.S. whitetail hunters spend in the woods each fall and early winter, comparing that tally to the number of Pope and Young book heads, and the returns on our investment in time are small.

This may surprise you, but I consider any whitetail a trophy. For the beginning hunter needing to fill a tag just to see what it's all about, that is the most true. As you spend more years in the woods and take more animals, you refine that to good antlers or trophy antlers.

Then, too, you have to consider the fact that not every area of the country grows book heads. Some areas have so much hunting pressure animals don't get a chance to grow up, or the soil doesn't have the right mineral contents, or the food is not good enough and/or abundant enough. In these areas, the trophy bucks simply are the biggest ones there. Many hunters need to settle for this, because not everyone can be lucky enough to live in the best trophy areas or be able to get to them frequently enough.

This works into the next category — **if you want to get the buster trophies, you spend your time where they are.** Simple as that. You adjust your hunting to fit your goals.

The key, anywhere, is to try to put it all together, to improve your odds. And that's what we're trying to do in this book — help you improve your odds.

• *Any whitetail is a trophy, especially the first couple when you're learning what it is all about. Bob's son Mark began his bowhunting success with this fine doe, below. But if you're going to hunt trophy bucks, you have to go where they live. Bob Fratzke points toward prime big buck habitat.*

Improving Your Odds

First, you have to analyze what, exactly, you want to do or how good you want to be at it or how much time you can spend at it. I used to go all-out. I considered myself a good waterfowl hunter, a good grouse hunter, a good pheasant hunter and all that. But when I got into bowhunting I figured if I wanted to do it well, the best way would be to cut way back on the other things or quit them. **Good bow hunting takes time.** I'd be out duck hunting, but I'd be thinking about bow hunting. Or I'd be bow hunting and thinking about duck hunting. I was doing ok in these things, but not to my satisfaction and most enjoyment. I guess I really wanted to hunt good whitetails.

I don't believe you can start out as a trophy hunter, because **there is a lot of bowhunting knowledge you can pick up only in the woods** . . . on the firing line, so to speak. You can read books like this one. You can read magazines. You can go to seminars, and you can talk to other bow-hunters. But the best that you can do is get well prepared, to have a fairly good idea what to do and what to look for and what to expect. Most things you pick up will be entirely useful to you in your hunting area, but not everything translates. There *are* regional and local differences. (However, you also can carry this idea of "differences" too far. I don't know how many times I've talked to guys about certain things basic to whitetails and whitetail hunting, and one of their first questions is "Yah, but will that work in my area?")

To gain the necessary knowledge, you have to take animals. You learn, at the very least, when to draw on an animal and when not. You learn what they do under certain conditions of weather and alarm or suspicion. You learn how they live.

You just can't learn if you're saving all your luck for that one shot at a trophy animal. Wait for that monster to be the first one, or nearly the first one, and I guarantee at least nine times out of ten you'll blow it.

Getting your feet wet without worrying about a trophy helps you learn tracking and trailing. Any time you get a chance, you ought to help track. You learn a lot, and it's fun. Sort of like unraveling a mystery.

Get involved with other hunters this way . . . to learn something. If somebody hits an animal and needs help, go help. Don't get in the way, though. Be a help, not a bother.

Now and then you'll run into bowhunters who don't shoot because they're afraid to miss, afraid they'll lose an expensive arrow, afraid of who knows what. That really translates into lack of confidence, which brings me back to the same thing . . nothing beats the experience of getting a couple of animals tagged. You can't kill an animal with a quiverful of arrows; at least one of them has to get into the air.

That experience will tell you how far to let an animal come in, what's too close and what's not close enough, what's a high percentage shot and what's a low percentage shot.

You'll learn, for instance, that when the animal is in good range — 20 yards or thereabouts — **take the first decent shot.** Don't wait for a better one. That very seldom happens. A lot of hunters just starting want to wait for that better shot, and they can all tell stories about the deer that didn't really seem spooked but somehow managed to keep brush or saplings or something between them and the hunter, and there just never was a shot opportunity. And all of a sudden the deer was gone.

You need to know whether your camo clothing is right, whether your equipment is silent, how and when to move . . . all sorts of things, the countless details that must fall into place if you're to take a whitetail. Because if something can go wrong, it will. You want to iron out those problems on animals that won't have so much tension surrounding their taking.

• *Fratzke is adept in the woods and on the field and target ranges. To be consistently successful, a bowhunter needs to be able to find the deer and then hit them solidly when he finds them.*

4

• Bob Fratzke and his father, on the right path in 1963.

Just remember, nobody begins playing baseball in the major leagues . . . and not many people get up there, either. It takes work and more work.

Successful trophy whitetail hunting takes work and more work and clear thinking and time in the woods. You must pay your dues.

The Right Attitude

The right attitude is more important than anything else. You get that right attitude from proper scouting, proper equipment preparation, proper practice, proper hunting technique. You know what you can hit at 20 yards or thereabouts. So that's a positive item that clicks into place. **But** you don't rely on that shooting ability as a crutch. Even before that, you have to do all things right to get the animal into range, or let it get into range.

That comes with having the confidence in yourself and the stand or stands you picked out. Without that confidence in your stand and yourself, you won't be able to stand for five or six hours; you'll be thinking, "Maybe I should be over there . . . or there . . . or there."

Have confidence in your ability to select the best possible stand for that given area, and this will give you more confidence because you'll know that you're going to have more shots passing you at 20 yards than if you moved over another 50 yards. Fifty yards in the wrong direction can do more than reduce the number of good shots. It can keep you from seeing deer, which would do absolutely no good for your confidence or for your open tag.

You have reasoning and thought ability working for you, if you use it. Do the early scouting. Figure things out.

There's a lot of difference between knowing, wondering and hoping. If you take the time to do the prep work right, you'll know.

• *Accept your hunting tool's limitations and learn to hunt well enough to place yourself in the right position for a good shot at an unalarmed animal.*

Define Goals

Accepting The Hunting Tool's Limitations

I don't have any negative attitude about the fact that a bow is a limited range tool shooting a slow projectile (200 to 210 fps is **not** fast, when you compare it to a typical deer rifle bullet speed).

Why should I have **any** negative thoughts? Why should you? We selected the tool we're hunting with; it wasn't forced on us. If we do our scouting well, we know that the deer is going to move past us at right around 20 yards. You know that at that range you can put the arrow where you want it, unless you've wound your mainspring too tight with anticipation. (I get the dry heaves after a shot, but before the shot I'm allright. I sure know the excitement is there. If it wasn't, I most likely wouldn't be a trophy hunter, or a hunter of any kind.)

Confidence . . .

You won't be shooting through brush because you will have prepared shooting lanes when necessary. You're going to have your stand positioned right in relation to the approach of the deer and in relation to the best position for drawing and shooting undetected. No negative thinking here.

You're simply setting up to be most effective with the hunting tool you're using, under conditions that you accepted from the beginning. You're a long way past simply finding a deer trail, setting up and hoping something comes along.

Hunting a Specific Animal

Hunting a specific whitetail probably is one of the hardest things to do. I've taken most of my big racks the first time I saw them during the hunt. A lot of other successful whitetail trophy hunters are the same.

Whitetails have general patterns, but they don't have set patterns. Not the big ones, anyway. That's how they got that big.

Turn the situation around. If you were to look for the biggest, strongest human example, first you'd probably look for the busiest stop-and-go intersection in a big city. That's reasonable, because that's where you'd see the most people.

Then you'd learn that it might not be all that reasonable because there might be too much stress, too much crowding, not enough food, not enough of the range of necessary conditions. So you might shift to a place which wouldn't have as many people, where there might be more food, better food, less stress, fewer opportunities to be run over by a car or hit by a train, chance for more exercise and training. So you'd look for places which had these conditions in good concentrations, and that's where you'd expect to find the best physical examples of humans.

Something like college athletic areas, or fitness centers . . . little pockets here and there with the right conditions. You get the idea.

I sure don't set out to hunt a particular animal. **I set out to hunt nice**

bucks in a given area. They aren't so isolated that you'll find only one here and one half a county away. They run together now and then, and their territories overlap. In the rut, of course, there's even more chance of seeing good bucks if you have picked out a good area and a good stand location.

I know within a period of one hunting season I'm going to have at least one shot at a trophy animal. I have that much faith in my homework and in the area I have selected; I have to have that faith, because the signs are all there.

That one shot is all any hunter can ask. That's how restricted it is. If you do your homework right, if you get one shot at a trophy animal, you can give yourself a pat on the back, because a lot of times even that one shot doesn't happen, even when you're set up right.

If you blow the shot, don't plan on getting a shot at him again, though. That's almost impossible.

Solving For Success

The woods and the sign it contains are really just a big puzzle, a riddle. We're trying to figure out that riddle so we can tag trophies on a consistent basis. We're solving for success.

Far too many hunters — any hunters, not just whitetail bowhunters — get their priorities out of whack. **They spend far too much time honing their shooting abilities and far too little time in the woods figuring things out.** And when they are in the woods, they don't have an open mind. You

• To solve the whitetail riddle for trophy success, it helps to select the right area. This buck was only 18 months old, yet it already owned a fine rack. Good feed and good genetics create that swift start toward trophy status.

Define Goals

• Start your scouting early. Fratzke and Gary Bauer are checking a scrape and related trails in the spring, long before season begins.

have to look and see, then assess what the sign tells you. Shooting skill is an important part, but you cannot expect to use it as a crutch to make up for hunting skill deficiencies.

I enjoy target shooting, but I would guess 90 percent of the bow-hunters around are not target archers. I enjoy it because I like to have a bow in my hand all year. I shoot a target bow, with target equipment. Since I shoot instinctively, I get plenty of practice at judging distance. **You'll notice that I emphasize the 20-yard distance. That's because it's not too close and it's not too far.** It's the distance which you can usually be deadly accurate at, and not so close that any tiny item will spook the deer, not so close there's too much tension.

Most hunters wait until way too late to do their scouting. They want a big buck, but they don't know where to start looking for big bucks. You can roughly pattern big buck movements in any good area, and you can do this in the fall . . . but you can't do it unless you have found the right area first. Finding that right area is best done at other times of the year, which we will get into soon.

Most hunters wait until a week or two weeks before season to do their scouting. They don't have any idea what the inside of the woods really looks like. So they're goofing up an excellent part of the season (the first couple of days of bow season can be excellent for bucks, even trophy bucks) by hunting the wrong spots in the first place, alerting the deer in the area as they move and scout or place themselves out of position.

Keep An Open Mind

I mentioned this earlier, but it is worth emphasizing. Keep an open mind and see what you're looking at, not what your mind wants you to see. Even when you're just walking through the woods. Some people can walk for miles and not see a tenth of the sign someone else will see in a couple hundred yards . . . in the same terrain.

Remember that when you're scouting during hunting season you have two purposes . . . scouting and hunting. That doesn't help your concentration and success with either. You have to decide to fish or cut bait. You may look where you saw deer last year or the year before. You may not notice that an area might be opened up a bit in a woods interior, or downfalls have blocked a big control path or trail. Dutch elm disease has indirectly affected deer movement in this manner. Soil erosion and ditches, either appearing or disappearing, affect deer movement patterns.

Details . . . details . . . details. Look for them. Look for them and see them, in the right time and with an open mind. Make notes. Go to school, really. Learn.

Those whitetails are full-time whitetails. We're only part-time hunters. They have a big jump on us. Joe Louis said of one of his boxing opponents; "He can run, but he can't hide." Well, the whitetail can run, he can hide, and he can go where and when he darned well pleases.

• *When you're hunting far from home, you usually won't be choosy. Sherwood Schoch, from Pennsylvania, took this big forkie in Minnesota. Fratzke said it was the only forkie buck in southern Minnesota.*

Define Goals

• *Notice how clearly the deer trails show on an early winter fly-over . . . clues for you to plug into your scouting/hunting analysis.*

Chapter 2
Scouting Year-Round

There are excellent reasons for scouting all year. Since following it on a calendar basis doesn't make sense, we're going to start with the end of the early season and go through the next early season. In my area, this will be from mid-November to mid-November.

Scouting year round keeps you familiar with the animals and their habitat, but it does more. That's because December and early spring right after the snowmelt are two of the best times to scout. At least, they are in any area of the snowbelt, and the general principles will work anywhere even though there's no snow.

Whitetails have different habits or patterns — in the spring, coming into early summer, once the season begins, within the season, right after the season.

Yeah, it's a lot of work, but it's worth it. Continual scouting is *not* a waste of time or energy.

First, you *know* what's in the area. That does a lot for your confidence and hunting opportunities and ought to do a lot for your shooting opportunities. You'll find that with continual scouting *you* will change *your* habits. You'll find yourself continually looking at feed and weather and cover and telling yourself deer will do this or that, or won't do it, and then you'll go check. The whole thing gets to be a passion, more than a game.

Spend enough time in the woods the right way and at the right time and you'll see enough deer to give you the confidence to feel "I've got a chance at a good one." If you just see some tracks on a few trails, catch a flag here and there, maybe get a lucky glimpse at one good buck, you can't have the necessary confidence.

To cap all this, can you think of a better way to enjoy a year than by spending a good bit of it outdoors doing something you really enjoy? It becomes a part of you and you become a part of it. Even the incidental bird sightings, small game sightings, weather conditions . . . the things you observe and make a part of your memory bank go far beyond simply categorizing deer information. Those things add to the basic efforts. **When you learn enough to see the relationships, to know what's going to happen by picking up information bits from other wildlife and the feel of things, that's when it gets to be most rewarding.** Your understanding level is higher, you're more of a participant than a befuddled observer.

• *Fratzke and Dave Morrison hunt with bows during the rifle season (legal in Minnesota) because they learn the deer's primary escape and cover trails and locations. This is orange camouflage.*

Don't Misread Kill Totals

If you're looking for the best place to hunt good deer, you have to define "best." If you want to go where the kill totals are highest, get a report from the DNR and look at the county listings. But recognize that you'll also have the most hunters breathing down your neck there, too.

Those seldom are the places to find good bucks or trophy bucks. The deer don't get a chance to mature. A buck generally spends the first 2½ years of its life growing up in body. Only when that is fulfilled does he really start pouring the coals to antler growth. If conditions are right, he can get pretty good antlers while he's also filling out and growing up, but that doesn't happen too often.

If you want trophy buck areas, look at the Pope and Young Record Book listings, look at state listings, check newspaper reports and talk with other bowhunters. Check DNR kill records where deer have been aged. Look at soil maps, too, to get an idea where the soils with high mineral content are. Try to pick up on any correlations that might begin showing a pattern.

The reason you can't go solely on sighting reports is that darned good bucks can live in an area for years and few people will see them. If those few who do see them are hunters, you might not hear much about those sightings.

If you want trophy hunting, you're better off hunting a trophy area only 10 times a year than hunting every day in an area where there "might" be a good one or two.

• Dave Schroeder, a Michigan bowhunter, took this fine trophy as it moved out of a thicket on the edge of an open field . . . a matter of being in the right place at the right time and capitalizing on it.

You can hunt an area with forkies and six-pointers all your life and never see a trophy, much less kill one. But if you learn an area with trophy bucks and study it well, you ought to be able to get a shot at a trophy buck in one of those 10 times. I don't believe expecting one shot at a trophy is too high an expectation, especially if you've done your homework. I expect to get at least one shot at a trophy buck each year.

My type of hunting is 90 percent scouting and only 10 percent hunting. I don't waste hunting time in the woods wishing and hoping, standing here and there on a trial basis. I find the spots, learn to hunt them, get set up, and then go in and expect to get my shot. There's no reason you can't do and expect the same. Ten times in a good area, where you have done your homework, ought to be enough saturation of hunting time to get that shot!

Know the Land

If you're going to be successful consistently, this is an important factor. You obviously need to know whitetails, too, but if you know the land that's half of the puzzle. You can know whitetails and have a very good idea of what to predict, but the **terrain almost always has small variations that you need to get to know.** As I've said before, "close" and "almost" aren't good enough. You can be 50 yards away from an excellent position and not realize it until you go look for it.

This is why I stress scouting in the spring. It gives you the time to be able to do it well. That way you know every trail, every rub, every scrape. They might move from year to year a little bit in particular areas but will still be dealing with the same general areas.

You will find primary scrape areas. They will be basically in the same areas, if not in exactly the same area. This tells you there is a reason, or reasons, for that location, so study the area. Notice the terrain, day winds and thermals, directions deer will be moving into and out of this area, time or times they move, where it is in relation to their movement to and from food sources. Look for the easiest route to travel. Ask yourself "Why?" constantly . . . not just in this scouting, but all the time you're scouting or hunting. When it comes to life habits, I don't believe they do anything "just because." **There has to be a reason or reasons, even though we often can't figure out what they are.**

Relative to primary scrape areas, you'll often find them as the hub of action, instead of an extended line. Generally, the primary scrape is in or near the center, but this doesn't always happen. That scrape usually will be a corker. I hunt near one area that looks like a barnyard. It must be 60 feet square and everything is torn up. The actual scrape is about eight feet by eight feet.

Knowledge of the terrain helps in additional ways, I've found. For instance, when I get a hit, I have a good idea where the animal is going to

• Scout with a plan and a purpose. This begins with map and platbook checking to determine the land you want to scout/hunt and to find out who owns it.

travel after he is hit. Even if I didn't see him or can't find the blood trail, I can still follow him with a fair degree of certainty. That just helps my odds for recovering that animal.

Knowledge of the terrain has helped me a lot of times when dragging a deer back out. They like to go down the slope in my area and into some real thick cover. If they get far, dragging a decent-sized buck up and out is work. I can either leave the deer where I field dress it, then go back in the next morning and drag it out the easiest way or I can drag it out that night through a shortcut I know or to a road access that is much closer than the way I walked in while trailing the animal.

Scout With a Purpose

Any good deer hunter scouts with a purpose and a strategy. That person may look like he's merely walking around out there in the fields and woods and swamps, but he's absorbing more than most people can be shown.

That's what my spring scouting is, for the most part. More on this later in this chapter.

You have to use your intellect and reasoning, but you have to **do it openmindedly.** You have to try to do it like a deer does — when he knows there's something wrong with an area, he just gets the hell out of that area and then circles under cover to see what it was all about. Sometimes that circling gets him in trouble, but at least he made the right first move.

You should be able to do that, too. When your sixth sense tells you to do something, do it. I've done enough scouting and deer taking, and been proven right enough times (even if you're consistently wrong enough times, you ought to be able to look at the flip side of the situation and maybe figure out what the right thing is) that I trust my sixth sense. I depend on it, on my hunches, a lot. **After I see what the deer will do, or generally will do, then I can set up like the predator I am.**

I can be in a tree stand one morning and tell myself, "Well, I'll hunt this for an hour into the day, then move to that other treestand over there." I'm not scared to move. Something tells me these things. I think it's mostly a result of a lot of intense work, so a lot of hunting hints are buried in my subconscious and they pop up without my thinking of them. That's the "lucky" part. I've seen enough deer movements and actions in countless different situations, so some sort of mental computer brings up the necessary information when my conscious and subconscious recognize enough key conditions or signs.

Once you have done enough scouting and hunting homework, you'll see the same patterns developing, the same responses. I think a person should play his hunches. Don't be scared to do something like that. The little signs like wind shifts or type of day or slight change in the weather which might get deer up and feeding, or whatever . . . those are the things which tell you, almost without thinking, to make a change. The deer movement patterns and trends you've seen in similar past experiences help decide what to do and when to do it.

Similarly, you'll be able to call up this information to help find signs. A couple of years ago I walked into a location and knew the rutting area just had to be in there somewhere. It took a little checking, and we eventually walked right into it. I doubt whether I would have found it, or thought to look for it, without adequate prior experience.

I cleared out the brush and branches from the stand locations I selected. Next fall I'm going to go down there and spend a couple of mornings and I *know* I can take a good buck there. It's a natural.

It's down in the bottom, where about four valleys funnel together. Most of the better primary scrape areas and breeding areas in my area are in valley bottoms or nearly on the valley floor. (Some are on ridge tops and on the edges of isolated high fields.)

Thermals will be moving down in the morning darkness, but the best way for me is to go right down in there and let the thermals move my scent ahead of me a little. I can get in fast and quiet that way, which is more valuable than worrying about coming in from downwind. Once I get set up, the thermals will drain my scent off down the valley through the fields, so that will be ok.

Besides, I'm going to hunt it only during the rut. This means I really don't need to worry about moving anything out of there as I come in. Whatever I move out will be replaced soon by more deer moving through. **A lot of hunters worry about spooking deer as they come into an area, but during the rut when deer are always on the move this should be one of your lesser concerns.**

My guess is that deer probably won't be there anyway when I come in to that stand. It will be quite early, so they most likely will still be feeding, if they're feeding. They will be feeding someplace else, not there.

When bucks start chasing does, they're going to go where they always go — the paths of least resistance. That will bring them past me at the natural hub of their movements.

Necessity of an Open Mind

Too many hunters handicap themselves with preconceived notions. They have rules of thumb fixed in their mind, then set out to find signs which verify those preconceptions.

Experience is invaluable, but you must always keep an open mind, be flexible, see what is there instead of what you want to see.

Everyone talks about competitive archery being 95 percent mental. **Bowhunting** is the same.

November

In Minnesota, we can bowhunt deer during the gun season. That begins around the end of the second week of November. It's a prime time to be out there with the bow because the bucks are still in rut. It's my main time to get a good shot at a buck. Oddly enough, there are so many meat hunters in existence that there isn't the pressure I expected. We have a lot of "hunters" who would rather wait for the special hunt at the end of the season which is a three-day, either-sex event. They feel more sure about getting a deer . . . even though they would have 10 days, 10 prime days of buck rut, just before that. Shows you how little a lot of people either know about deer hunting or care about good bucks.

During this hunt — and I think in most every firearm season anywhere — I can go out during the middle of the week and encounter zero hunters. If I do see hunters, they're usually of the two-hours-in-the-morning/two-hours-in-the-evening variety. They're leaving their stands before they should because they're antsy, cold, or don't know they shouldn't.

• *To be successful, you must spend time in the woods. Many people will be moving out for lunch at this time. They move deer. Where will you be at that time? (Already back in camp, if your morning hunt was successful.)*

Since deer generally move all day long at that time of year, I can stay out there all day, hunt how and where I want, and not have to worry about hunting pressure.

The prime benefit of hunting during the heavy pressure of, say, opening weekend, is that you get the best chance of the year to see their primary escape routes. With that many people in the woods, moving as much as they always do, the deer are either going to head for their number one cover or get the hell out of the area to someplace with better cover.

Even though I may not have hunted much on any of these primary routes earlier in the season, I will have scouted them out during the previous spring or some other time. I will know **exactly** how the terrain looks in a given area. So I know just by looking at it, analyzing it, using some common sense . . . if a deer comes down off that hill, for instance, where he's going to go for a shortcut out of there, because of the hunting pressure, and where I should be situated.

If you haven't done that same type of homework in your area, you can't pick out the right stand spots. **A whitetail doesn't need much cover or variation in the terrain to run or sneak past you, so you have to know the details.** A distance of 50 feet can put you in the ballgame or completely out of the ballpark. You want to be able to recognize the right place, not just a "somewhere in here" location.

The added hunting pressure adds another benefit — it concentrates the activity for you, saves you a lot of work. Not all deer will travel primary routes. They will head out on secondary routes, too. If you have done enough looking around in advance, then do enough now, you ought to be able to get a good evaluation by the number of tracks, directions they traveled, when they traveled, etc.

You'll also probably find back door routes you might have missed earlier. **Bucks sort of drift through areas.** They aren't as trail oriented as does and fawns, not even when the terrain limits their movement in certain areas. For instances, if there's a slight depression or draw through a thicket, you'll find them moving through that lower area somewhere. But don't look for a distinct trail.

This is the time to check loose clusters of tracks, see whether they were made together or singly, see how each deer moved, backtrack to see where it came from and why, or follow it to see where it went. Backtracking is an excellent learning tool. You can see how the deer lived, where it lived, and with clear thinking you should figure out why it did what it did. However, in many areas of good deer population, backtracking is difficult at best, impossible at worst, because there are too many overlapping tracks in certain areas (hubs of movement) to enable you to stay on an individual track. Do the best you can; there's always more to learn.

If the peak of the hunting pressure and the rut coincide, I wouldn't be too concerned about feeding animals or picking out spots where feeding is occurring, because if any does are coming into heat you're going to see bucks. I would hunt where I know does are going to move past. Even though a buck will stick with a doe for the day or so she's receptive (plus several hours before and after) and maybe wander off the main trail or move very little, **my chances are mathematically better if I'm positioned where the most does will be moving.** After all, they can't all come into heat at once and run back in the woods *en masse,* even though the sudden flurry of activity when the peak of the rut occurs sometimes make it look that way.

For new scouting during the firearms season, the best bet probably would be to wait and walk it at the close of the season, unless there's been a warm spell melting snow and wiping out good sign. I'm a stand hunter. I don't like to walk all over the country during good hunting time, especially during the rut. I'd move myself out of far more good situations than I'd ever move myself into. Plus, there would be just that much more opportunity to create additional stress.

At the end of season, or shortly after the end of the heavy hunting pressure if that ends before season ends, deer are going to be pushed into their best hiding spots, where they feel safest. This can be the thickest cover, roughest terrain, furthest from roads, game refuges or all those unobvious places like a brush thicket behind a shed or a small patch too out in the open (in the hunter's humble opinion) for a self-respecting deer to hide.

Evaluate where the human pressure has been to find where else the deer will be.

Finding these places at the conclusion of the firearm season or shortly after it tells you that the deer are here for a long-term preference, as opposed to having been pushed there a couple of hours ago, then possibly pushed out of there by more hunter movement a couple of hours later.

At the end of the season, you can go into these heavy cover areas, count the beds, look at the entry and exit trails, things like that. When you're examining deer beds, buck beds have the urine stain in the middle of the bed while doe urine stains are on the edge of the bed or just outside it.

Note where the beds are in relation to prevailing winds, ridgetops, dropoffs, cliffs, swamp edges, thickets, draws (and other quick escape routes). Note how much and how far deer can see from their beds. Remember that most water is not a barrier to deer, but it is to us. Widest rivers and lakes obviously won't be crossed as readily, but deer don't hesitate to swim. A big body of water can provide as much protection for a deer as an open field it can see across; but you can turn this same information to your advantage, knowing that deer will travel around the edges of these big, open areas, probably on the upwind side so their nose can give them protection from upwind and their eyes can give them protection downwind.

Game animals like to take the path of least resistance most of the time, unless, for instance, a trail goes up the side of a depression which keeps them hidden. Even then, they'll break out of it as soon as they figure they're safe and move on a less-steep path.

Seems like hunters either hunt the easiest spots or go out to the most remote spot . . . drive as far as they can and ignore all the area between. That in-between area is where the deer usually end up, simply because they avoid the pressure.

December

Whitetails will basically keep those same general bedding areas unless the weather gets really mild or if they're too far from winter feed. If the weather gets colder, they'll stay in the heavy cover out of the wind, and travel farther to feed if they have to.

I don't believe there's much difference in their feeding intensity right after firearm season. When they go hungry, it's because of the rut not because of hunting pressure. At that time of year, the nights are long so there's plenty of time for them to feed then during the firearm season.

Also, a deer won't even hesitate to travel two miles then or later in the winter to feed. That's a lot of movement, which means that you ought to be able to have a lot of places to set up during the late season and catch them between feeding and bedding areas.

• *Cross-country skiis help you cover ground better than walking. Enjoyable winter exercise and another scouting jaunt, all rolled together.*

Scouting now can be good for several reasons: 1) crops have essentially been harvested, so there's less for them to hide in (corn, for instance) and the feeding areas are concentrated; 2) concentrated feeding areas probably will be used all winter, so you will have a chance now to check and double check approach and departure trails; 3) foliage, except for some leafy oak brush, is gone and deer will be more visible, especially with a snow cover on the ground (brown against white is one of my favorite color combinations); 4) toward the end of this time, especially if the snow gets deeper, there will be a yarding effect. That's when you'll see what the migrating whitetails do in your area. It may not be anything, or it may be a few miles. Either way, you want to know.

In the far north, you'll see some huge yards. Further south, down into the more open, farming country, all this means is that the deer remaining in the area after the hunting season will group together. In my area, there probably will be extended family groups of 20 to 35 animals, and they will cover a valley region of maybe five to six miles. **These groups will have big bucks.**

If you get around enough, you ought to be able to locate these herds. This will give you an idea of how many animals remain and whether there are any trophy bucks. They will have their antlers yet. The big ones will, anyway. From what I've seen, the big ones won't drop their antlers until close to the end of December, after the small mid-December last rut.

The dominant bucks are going to compete to breed the few remaining does not bred in November as those does come into estrus again around mid-December. Those bucks will be on the prod, which keeps them more visible, less wary. You'll be able to see where they're moving and where they have been. You'll hope to find out where they're bedding down if they're bedding down.

To start your search, go to the feed source or sources. In my area, this usually is corn. Ripe corn doesn't always need to be harvested in the fall, so if the farmer doesn't have storage space or the corn's moisture content was too high or the field was too wet to get into, he's likely to leave it until spring. Since corn is high energy feed, it is excellent winter feed for animals. This winter supply also can be soybeans, an uncut hay field, whatever. Even if the corn has been picked, there will be plenty of shelled corn and missed ears on the ground. Deer don't miss them. Did you ever notice, too, how quickly any pheasants in the area will find that corn?

The deer will stay fairly close to their feed source(s) if they can. That's only logical, especially in winter when they would want to expend as little energy as possible.

They *will* go across open fields to get to their feed source. They take the easiest route. Even if they are exposed, it is only briefly.

They move early but also will move later into the morning, and they will move earlier in the afternoon. It's warmer during daylight hours, so they use less energy while traveling. Also, since there's less hunting pressure they have less of a reason to move at night or closer to dusk and daylight.

You should see a lot of animals at this time of year, and you should be able to do best in the morning. The two bucks on the cover were taken December 16, 1978, just a few miles from each other. I took mine at 7:30 a.m. It was chasing one doe. Len Anglewitz took his at 4 p.m. It was chasing eight does. My hunting partner, Dave Morrison, missed one at 35 yards at 7:45 a.m. It had a narrower but higher rack than Len's. It was alone and really windmilling. Mort said I spooked it when I left my stand to dress out my buck. So Mort had to take the photo of us instead of being in it. We've always thanked him for his ability to take a nice photo.

Your scouting and hunting now unavoidably run together. You're basically hunting now but scouting simply because you're in the area, observing what all goes on. You're scouting for tomorrow, next week, next year. If you find you aren't quite in the right place, you can adjust tomorrow and clear out a new area for next week or next year. As far as I'm concerned, you never have too many places to hunt, never have too many good stands . . . and you always scout with more than the immediate future in mind.

With your scouting, the closer you can determine the bedding locations, the better off you are. This is because the return trails from feeding to bedding areas funnel in. If you set up halfway between a feeding and bedding area, you're effectively (or ineffectively) part way up the funnel. You'll miss seeing a lot of animals or be out of range if you do see them. The closer you are to the bedding area, the narrower the funnel. This is for winter, when deer are bunched more. Earlier in the season, there is more of an hour-glass effect in the trails, with deer spreading out again when they get near their bedding areas. This means that in early season you will want to be positioned a bit further from the beds so you can see most deer movement in the narrowest part of the hour-glass pattern.

Naturally, if those deer took the same trail or trails back every day they wouldn't last long. Maybe they move on different trails by pure choice, but wind direction, hunting pressure, or other conditions will help them (and *you*) decide which trail to use. Be aware they will sometimes move in what at first seem dumb patterns, such as right across an open field. I've found this open field maneuver more of a late season trick than an early season one, because they have fewer good, protected bedding areas and they often go directly to them as a means of expending less energy.

They will generally begin moving just before daylight, probably doing most of their traveling then. You have to be able to set up in the dark far enough ahead of them that you won't spook them. This is another reason to get as close to their bedding area as possible — you'll probably be

• A genuine bull-of-the-woods most likely made this rub. Not only is the rub large, the tree is gouged deeply . . . indications of a good-sized buck.

further from the deer when you come in.

It will be cold as the devil sometimes on a dark, starry December morning, but you're much better off being an hour early than a minute late. I've found that, when going in that early, deer often are bedded down along some brush or out in a field (down off the top, out of the wind). I've been able to walk past them within 15 feet and not have them spook. I'm quiet and make no threatening moves, so if they pay any attention they just watch me walk past. Since some deer may be moving then, small movement sounds shouldn't be alarming.

You might want to check feeding areas outside of refuge or other protected areas and follow the trails to those protected areas. Deer aren't naive after they've been hassled. They know where those areas are, and I think sometimes they know exactly how far a specific bow or specific firearm is effective. They seem to be just beyond that distance most of the time when you see them.

When you're looking for the best place to set up, keep a hockey net in mind. You're the goalie, and all you're doing is trying to cut down the angle of that hockey puck buck shooting toward the net of cover.

Fly the Area

Flying over an area is one of the most overlooked, one of the most effective, one of the least expensive ways of scouting that I know. Flying time, on a per hour basis, is expensive, but when you think of all the terrain you can cover in that short time, all the auto and truck gas you save, it becomes cheap. If you can find a pilot who is looking for any excuse to take a plane up, you might be able to get by for even less money than usual. I prefer flying with pilots who don't hunt, for obvious reasons. If I can't find one like that, I don't make evaluative comments in flight — I might find him in my stand next fall.

Fly all the area, over standing corn, other agricultural crop fields or other feeding areas (oak ridges can be good until the snow gets too deep). Fly over bedding areas and all areas between feeding and bedding. In short, look over the whole country.

You would be surprised how, even from the air, you can see the trails between these areas. Take photographs of everything, then analyze the photos later.

Flying cuts down on scouting time, and every time you move through snow on foot, it takes time and energy. There's nothing wrong with getting a little fresh air while you do some snowshoeing or cross-country skiing, but it can be colder than cold at times. Windy, too.

When you're flying, have the pilot tip the plane a bit so you can take a better photo. You can shoot right through the window on most planes. If not, the pilot probably will let you open the window.

(Editor's Note: If you try this, shoot at 1/500th of a second or faster or else you will have a large collection of blurred photos. Bracket your exposures — shoot at three or four f/stop settings to be sure you have something. Photography over snow is a lot like photography over water, because there is extra light reflection coming off the surface of that water or snow.)

You'll be able to see where the deer moved to a wintering location. File that information, because next year you may be able to set up along a migration route and do alright.

This also is an excellent way to discover all the terrain changes and get the best over-view of the entire terrain to see the relationships of why deer may move from one area to another. Small changes in terrain or cover may seem insignificant to you, but they won't be insignificant to the deer. This gets back to seeing instead of just looking.

For instance, my area has a lot of ridges that are farmed at the top. Ridge sides are wooded. Valley bottoms are farmed. Every once in a while a little gulley will begin at the edge of a ridgetop field. That erosion is inevitable. This erosion also changes deer routes. If they want to parallel a hillside they don't like to go through these deep depressions. They either will cut down below one or break out over the top just before the gulley.

So if you're hunting halfway between, you're missing the whole ball-game.

These things usually are visible from the air. Then you can check them in your pictures and double check by inspecting them on foot.

When you're flying, take a map with you, preferably a topographical map. Mark the map with film roll number (assuming you shoot more than one roll) and frame number. You'll need these keys, because a handful of photos can sometimes be deceiving. Some will be easy to pinpoint, but some won't.

Analyzing Your Photos

You'll be able to mark the perimeter trail following around the openings, back in the brush 20 yards or so. There will be depressions or thickets which will be points of emergence for deer onto the field, to feed or to cross it. There will be approach trails and bedding areas back behind the perimeter trail.

Since you know where the deer are and will be before and during pressure situations, you can analyze the terrain and see where they will be most likely to go when pushed. They generally go the route of least resistance. They like to travel in the semi-open, such as right along a thicket or swamp, or just below a ridgetop so their body will be hidden yet they can see quite a distance. This is easier moving, yet it is right next to instant dense cover. **Easier moving also means quieter moving.**

The pressure situations change things, force the deer to choose. That's where your scouting and analyzing skills come into play. On a ridgetop, for instance, the direct route over the top may be exposed — as I noted earlier — but it also may mean less traveling, very brief exposure, less predictability (if the hunter figures they will stay in the brush and circle the ridge), and fastest means to heaviest cover. You sure aren't going to follow those deer anywhere — their legs are an excellent defense here. They can be across a hundred-yard field in just a few seconds, and they will be moving. Even for a rifleman that may not present much of a shot — wide open ridgetops have more dips and shallow depressions than you believe, until you stand back and take a clear look. One of those little dips can cover a deer for a long way, especially if you're out of position.

Often this isn't enough, though, even in shotgun-only areas. **I think nowadays the deer that are runners are dead. The ones that are sitters and hiders are the survivors.** They're letting you walk right by them. The ones with the best nerves win.

What happens is that deer are harrassed from the time the hunting season starts by bow hunters, grouse hunters, squirrel hunters, hikers, gun hunters, and so on. We have patterns, too, so it stands to reason that deer know basically what to expect. They know how and where to stay put. If they had to run every time someone stepped into the woods and they detected it, they wouldn't ever have time to rest.

I'd guess we're probably walking past 90 percent of the deer we eventually get a shot at. In the mornings, I won't hesitate to go out to my stand in the dark. As long as they don't smell you, and you're taking your time and not crashing through brush, they don't know what you are.

Since you keep moving and aren't directly threatening, you soon move on out of their area of concern and they relax again. Every time that happens to a deer, it becomes more certain that that is the best way for it to survive.

I feel very comfortable going into the woods in the dark and getting set up on stand. This comes back to the need to get there early enough.

One particular November morning I was going to one of my favorite treestands down in the valley. I got there a little bit later in the morning than I like; it was almost breaking day. I got set up in the treestand and I knew I had kicked something out of there on the way in.

I was among a big scrape line. About an hour and half later, here came a nice eight-pointer, right down the trail with his nose to the ground. He was on a hot doe trail.

I had two shooting lanes cleared out to cover the trail from the direction he was coming. The first lane was a bit head-on and not quite right for a behind-the-shoulder shot. The second lane would have the deer broadside, even quartering slightly away. Perfect.

So here came the buck, nose down, tracking just like a hound. He passed through the first shooting lane, and I waited for him to get into the second lane . . . looking, looking, looking . . he isn't there. He's going up the hill, back and forth, all the way up and over the hill.

Evidently, when I got in there a doe was already at the biggest scraping area, waiting for action. I pushed the doe out, and the buck followed the doe. He never knew I was there. He was 15 yards from me, but I never got a shot.

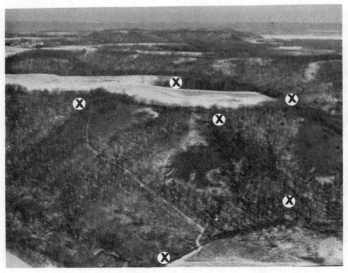

• The Xes mark good stand locations, high and low, where bucks tend to move through cover, check scrape areas or feed.

Main part of winter

This is the time to do your homework and research. Reintroduce yourself to your family and friends. After you've done that, here's a list of things you ought to consider:

- Check-up flyover
- Talk to farmers
- Scout new terrain
- Get herd information from the DNR and study it
- Read magazines and books on whitetail hunting to see if there's anything which will add to your knowledge, answer questions, fill in gaps
- Check on wintering herd health, available food supplies
- Check out stand locations for next late season
- Get out and enjoy the outdoors

Remember, the more work you do, the more time you spend in the woods, the more effectively you see what you're looking at and analyze what you're seeing, the luckier you'll get.

This time of year will be ideal for check-up flyovers. Take the camera and shoot another roll of film. Film is cheap, compared to all the other time and expenses you devote to whitetail hunting. Compare these photos with any you might have taken in the late hunting season.

Flyover will give you the best look at the terrain as I've noted earlier and want to emphasize. Now you can check herd size, degree of yarding, yarding effects, amount of movement to feeding areas. If you have DNR data on deer density in that area before the hunt, then compare that to herd sizes now, you can get a good idea of the kill percentage, and by looking at the severity of the winter and amount of food available you can also get a decent idea of fawning for next spring and next year's herd size and strength.

When you're noting available food and its location, you can check this next summer against crop locations and know whether deer will or will not be likely to be in the same area or moved slightly (or a lot). This can be a clue as to whether you will have good results hunting that area in next year's late season.

I use this time to combine looking at new land and talking to farmers. First, though, I'll go over topographical maps and plat books so I know what the country looks like (comparing photos to topo maps to pin down details) and who owns the land I want to inspect on foot.

I've tried walking through snow, and I've tried snowshoeing. That's why I have a pair of cross-country skis. I can have fun, get some exercise and cover quite a bit of ground, all as I scout for deer. If I get out often enough, it doesn't take long before I can pick up on some of the conditions which affect deer movement and feeding patterns. I can see how they respond to different weather conditions, what they eat and don't eat

• *A much younger Bob Fratzke engaged in a pleasant winter pastime.*

at various times and under various stress conditions — because any way you slice it, winter in the snowbelt can be and usually is a stress condition.

I've made notes during past seasons. I can update my notes, see what details I've overlooked or misinterpreted, and see whether my notes can answer some of my own questions.

Analyzing photos and comparing them to topo maps takes time. It also is a lot of fun. So I can't exactly say I'm "working hard" during winter evenings when I'm doing these things.

Since I do my own taxidermy on deer heads, this is another way to fill up the winter and keep the fever going.

Spring Scouting

After snow melt, before anything starts growing, the terrain looks basically like it does in the fall. Everything which happened immediately preceding the rut and during the rut itself is still recorded on the ground and, of course, in rubs.

In our part of the country, it usually snows around mid-November. That's just about the time the first and main rut is ending. Any appreciable snow covers all the signs which already exist, and any rutting activity which continues will also be recorded if the snow isn't too deep.

When the snow melts, you have a bare woods to look through to study terrain, and you have all the rutting activity there to study.

That's part of the reason spring scouting is excellent. Another reason is that when you're out there bowhunting in the fall, you either do not take time to scout or you tend to hurry it. You're bowhunting. You may be looking around, but you aren't really scouting. **So the spring gives you time to concentrate on scouting and analyzing sign and terrain.** I mean, really look it over to determine why deer move here and don't move there. Always ask yourself why they do such and such a thing.

You will be surprised, the first time you do it, how far you can see through the timber and brush. Since snow will have matted the leaves, every little change in terrain is visible. Trails will be most visible, too. The ground looks like it has been rolled with a lawn roller, and that's why all the little blips show up.

If you find the scrapes, why do the deer come into those areas to scrape? Are there more trails back up further which lead into the scrape area? **Look, see, think, analyze. Forget about any preconceived notions. Free your mind to concentrate on the situation, the open book, there in front of you.**

Since the trees are open, this also is the time to select and trim out your

---

• *Start your spring scouting by simply looking at the area and analyzing it as best you can. Then check the existing sign for verification. Patterns from the rut of the previous fall will be fresh right after the snow melts, and the woods will be open, just as it will be during the rut next fall.*

• *Photo taken from Fratzke's tree stand shows the fall trail clearly. Fratzke, in right of photo, checks feeder trails connecting with the main trail.*

exact treestand positions for the fall. Trees now look just as they will in the fall during rut. If there is any kind of cover to use now, you know there will be more cover for you on that tree in the fall because not all of the leaves will have fallen.

All fresh cuts will have aged by fall and won't be noticeable. A quicker way is simply to smear some mud or dirt on them. They look 10 years old immediately.

I'm certain a lot of hunters pick out their treestand location in August or September, then are amazed that the stand isn't worth a hoot in late October and early November. A treestand surrounded by August leaves is one thing; sticking out like a sore thumb two months later is another. They could be silhouetted, too close to a field, on trails not used any more for that season, etc.

• *Fratzke checks stand position, upper left, while Gary Bauer clears shooting lanes, upper right. Below, scrape shows in foreground. Bucks traveled along a dry creek bed and then turned up this old logging trail, noted by faint depression.*

• *Two views, one southeast and one northeast, from treestand. With the woods this open, every ripple in the landscape is open to scrutiny. The details are right there for you to analyze.*

You won't have a lot of time to do your spring scouting, so don't get lazy about it. You have to do it while the soil is still moist and the trails are most visible. Our photos were taken at two times, in mid-April and the first of May. In mid-April the trails were highly visible. The first of May, I didn't realize I was walking over trails until I found the primary scrape area. Then, after I looked again, I could see the impressions where they were coming out of a ditch and going up the side of a draw. I couldn't believe how many trails I had just walked over. I had walked too fast, not checking as thoroughly as I should have.

This same condition is noticeable after a light snowfall in early winter. Several deer will have moved through an area, but they will have moved independently and not on a specific trail. Without the snow, you would see no sign. The area, however, is excellent if hunted right.

Carry a compass on your spring scouting jaunts. When you're looking at trails and other signs, it's just as easy to forget direction then as when you're trailing a wounded buck. Not only will you keep your directions straight, which can prevent confusion later, you also can check prevailing winds and figure exactly where they will be during hunting season. Remember that prevailing wind direction shifts from spring to fall. Find out the direction and degree of shift in your area. This is vital if you're going to set up your stands in the best locations. Since winds shift from day to day, you'll make the necessary additional stand setups and tree clearing. They won't be used as often as the primary stand, but when they must be used they must be right.

You ought to prepare at least three stands in any given area, just to give yourself moving-around opportunities. You may or may not be surprised how winds/breezes can vary within 50 yards or so. That, again, is the reason for close scouting and paying attention to details at each location. That's why **it is dangerous to try to simplify setup, scouting and hunting position rules.** The key is what is happening in your exact locale, each individual stand location, not what generally will happen over the western half of the North American continent on relatively flat land. Rules of thumb can lead to broken thumbs.

If you think animals are approaching from a different direction than anticipated, moving 50 yards could mean a world of difference. Keep this in mind, even while you're sitting up in a tree stand. Don't be scared to change. Walk over there and do it, because you can do it. You have to remain flexible in your attitudes and actions, and you have to be confident in your conclusions and in yourself.

One time I spooked a deer as I went into a stand. This was on a windy, windy day. You can get away with a lot on windy days. I had climbed to the right height in my tree, had my tree stand in my hand and my bow hanging on a cutoff branch when two does came and stood right underneath me.

I stood there five minutes waiting for them to leave. They didn't, so I figured, "What have I got to lose?" and started putting in the stand. Took my rope around the tree, tied in the stand, tested it for solidity, climbed onto it, reached down and grabbed my bow, took an arrow out and nocked it, sat there a while holding it . . . and they're still below me, walking around a bit. So I drew on them, did some practice aiming, let down, hung my bow on a branch and stood there.

The deer eventually moved off, and I just watched them go. Crazy.

I was careful and quiet putting in the stand; it was windy, so my noises were covered; the deer were directly below me and thus less likely to spot my movement than if they had been out a way, where I would have been more in their field of vision. One thing they don't have is eyes in the top of their head. It just seems like it at times.

Shed Antlers

Shed antlers are a bonus to the hunter doing spring scouting. They are a keepsake, a memento. They can be good for rattling antlers when fixed up.

Best, though, is the fact that when you find a big set of shed antlers, or more frequently just a single shed because they seldom shed them at once, you know the buck will be around again this fall, probably bigger, unless something happens to him.

• Shed antlers are fun to collect, and they also show that some good bucks made it through the winter. They should be around again next fall.

Just Looking

Spring scouting is just looking and absorbing. Looking for new things, checking things from last fall.

In the spring, if you scout right, you ought to be able to see the forest *and* see the trees. A lot of deer hunters can't see the forest for the trees, in more ways than one.

I analyze the signs and the terrain, then pick whatever seems to be the best bet. I analyze the terrain more than anything — it is always there. If I lay the sign analysis over the terrain analysis I know when and where to go just about as well as I'm ever going to.

Early Summer / Summer

Everything is green, fully leafed and growing. Crops are up and, fortunately, the corn isn't too high yet. This is the time you want to begin evaluating the deer in the areas you plan to hunt.

Crop rotation and growth are important. **Crop rotation will change from year to year, and it will have a definite affect on deer and their movement patterns.** You need to take note of various crop locations if you're going to hunt there the first week or so of season, because the deer will still be coming to those fields to feed.

Later, when the alfalfa or soybeans or corn are gone, you'll be ready to shift with the deer. You can waste a lot of time and screw up what little hunting you will have, if you have to spend much time searching for the deer every time they adjust to a changing food supply (or foliage change, or whatever).

When you know where the crops are and how/where/when deer move to them, you can change your stand location correctly and immediately. One year of scouting won't give you the best info on this because you won't have the previous year's information, so **to get really specific you need to work on cumulative notes and experiences.**

Crops are different. Deer like some better than others. Because I have the information from past seasons, I know a cornfield, for instance, in one location will attract more deer than a cornfield in another location that isn't too far away. You can learn the same thing, if you work at it.

Don't wait until crops, especially corn, get too high. By July 4th, bucks should have a good enough rack to let you know how they're basically going to look in the fall, and you'd better be doing your looking now. After that time, corn generally is too tall and hides the deer. With daylight saving time, you can get out there with good light and do the necessary evaluating.

This works best with binoculars or a spotting scope from a pickup truck. You can travel farm roads and field paths (with permission). You won't tear up the farmer's fields, which is a point in your favor, and you

• Deer don't like to make scrapes in tall grass, but Fratzke has found you can persuade bucks to make scrapes where you want them. Here he has selected an oak tree just off a corn field and is trimming out a circle under an overhanging branch. The buck makes its own scrape, so it is completely natural.

• *Deer run a perimeter trail, marked just inside the woods around this ridge. Most of the traffic on this trail will be does, yearlings and young bucks. Big bucks, being more wary, tend to hang lower and come up onto the trail from protected locations. They stand in heavy cover back from the perimeter trail and case the joint before emerging at typical places marked with an X. Your stand, to be positioned correctly, will thus be back off the trail, on the opposite side from the field, so the bucks will be looking past you as they examine the situation. You'll also have better wind protection this way, for your scent will be further above them.*

won't drive in those areas on rainy days for the same reason. Tell the farmer when you'll be there, so he won't wonder about the vehicle messing around the back of his land. If something *does* happen to his field, you're going to get the blame for it unless he knows for certain that it wasn't you who did the damage.

If the crops aren't too high, you can cover at least twice the territory in an evening just by driving and looking, stopping to glass animals when you see them. You aren't going to disturb them much, if at all. They might move back into the woods, but they usually will be back out five or 10 minutes later and resume feeding.

The main thing is to cover enough area to know where you have a given amount of good bucks, so you know where to hunt.

Once the corn gets too high, it covers a good 50 percent of my general hunting area. **Corn is natural habitat for deer. They live in there more than we think they do.**

Sometimes you can climb up in an old windmill or an abandoned silo or a tree that is strategically placed to see a long way. There's one old silo I spot from once in a while that is fantastic. You can see for a year from it, and it even has grapevines growing up its exterior. You could use that thing as a picturesque fortress.

One good area to spot deer is an alfalfa field a couple of days after it has been cut. The new, green, tender regrowth must be like candy.

• *Do deer like corn? This mess wasn't made by a tractor or a runaway bull. Deer spend more time in corn than we generally realize.*

Scouting

• Erik Fratzke, Bob's son, points to a track made by a heavy deer. Note the track in the right foreground and another one midway between it and the one being pointed to. The deer is so big it is knock-kneed; the tracks point out from its line of travel.

Preseason Scouting

You just can't go out two or three weeks before season and zero in on a buck. You won't even know the deer herd as you should. You sure won't know the terrain, as I think we've explained.

Preseason scouting is the time when I most probably slack off. I know from my summer scouting where the good bucks are, and now I'm just probably spot checking on those bucks to see if they're keeping the habits I checked and pinpointed earlier.

For the best spot checking, I'll sit on a stand overlooking a complete ridge or check from ridges and roads with the truck. I'll go from the best vantage point of a wide area, then go in to see if the buck is coming out on A, B or C trail, how often he does it, where he goes when he leaves the field, etc. But with minimal presence in the woods. I don't want to disturb the deer at all; I want to wait until the first day of season, have him move through in his normal route, and then put my tag on him.

Pre-season scouting is probably the worst time to clear treestand sites and shooting lanes. Deer are going to notice that the cover has been modified, and you're going to leave some human odor. You're **forcing** them to change their habits.

Preseason scouting is not the time to get started, but if you have to make the best of a bad situation, it is better than nothing. Just go ahead and scout as best you can, using the information given earlier in this book, and try to stir up the area as little as possible. Concentrate on the major trails so you can get the best pattern of general deer movements, and then if you want to wait for a good buck you may have picked up enough details on stand location by then — and avoided the big buck hangouts — to be in a good position when the rut begins.

Patterning

Bucks in most areas won't move in regular, clockwork patterns. Their movement in most areas is roughly circular, simply because they come into an area on X trails and leave that area on Y trails, even if they're just going from bedding to feeding areas and vice versa. This limits their exposure, removes the predictability. They all have more than one bedding and feeding area, too, which lowers predictability even further.

So I doubt whether you could say "I saw a buck there two nights ago. He should be passing through again tonight." **There is a lot of wandering in deer movements.** Under the circumstances of trying to figure out and predict a buck's pattern, I believe weather, type of day, stress and other variable conditions have a major influence. A buck may want to go from point A to point B, but coon hunters push him off his path and he goes to point C to feed and bed down. A day or two later he may or may not reach point B. He doesn't need to. He doesn't need to be home for

• What can we say? This is a rather unusual treestand. It was three feet from a deer trail. A huge buck probably was blinded by the glare from the fresh lumber, ran into a tree and died on the spot. But we doubt it. Your stand ought to be just a bit less obvious, maybe a whole lot less obvious.

dinner. He doesn't have to meet anyone at a certain street corner at a specific time. He doesn't have to cross a field in a certain number of minutes. He just wants to exist in the best and safest manner. That's why the deer takes what is given to it and, I believe, reacts more than acts.

(You know yourself how a shot situation often works out the best when you don't force it, but wait out a deer and let its actions dictate what you do or don't do.) Hiding under a bush or in a thicket and letting a hunter walk right past within 10 yards is a form of reaction . . . inactive reaction, a non-response response.

A big buck is almost impossible to predict. He knows when there's hunting pressure or other people pressure, and he'll just change his pattern enough to get by. He's as adaptable as they come.

A yearling buck is pretty predictable. He doesn't have the experience the big buck does, and his system isn't geared as slow. He doesn't have the control of himself that a big buck does. Hunting a yearling buck is about like hunting any yearling.

The only times you can figure to pattern good bucks are in late summer before season opens while they are still in their summer movement patterns and during the late season when snow ground cover, absent foliage and less available food make them more visible, travel farther and give you a record of their movements.

A deer's range isn't that large. For it to survive as well as it does, and go unseen as much as it does, it has to have excellent survival instincts and training. **If it was easy to pattern, the whitetail would be only a memory instead of the number one big game animal.**

Food availability seems to be a key to how well defined or poorly defined the patterns are, except during rut. In my areas, there is so much food that patterns are loose. In an area with fewer food sources and/or terrain conditions which force them to be more habitual, I would expect it to be easier to pinpoint individual animals and good bucks.

Any time any type of restriction comes into play, the deer loses an option or two. You pick up a point or two, then, in your odds.

Since deer foods vary from area to area within a state, and from region to region, it pays to study food consumption reports. State DNRs often have such reports. There are popular literature and all sorts of biological reports to study. Make use of that information.

(Editor's Note: On an elk hunt in Colorado several years ago, my "guide" — in response to a question I asked him about various types of vegetation and whether they were elk food — replied, "Durned if I know. As far as I'm concerned, there's two kinds of plants — them that are pines, and them that aren't." This was not, needless to say, the best hunt I've ever been on.)

Morning Trails and Evening Trails

You read a lot about these two types of trails. They *do* exist, and I believe there's a way you can beat them. This is because they're not a total trail, just part of the overall hour glass configuration of a master system of trails.

Scratch out a map here, first noting the location of the food source and then the bedding area. Bring in main trail or trails out of the bedding area toward the feeding area, then split them off, a Y fork in the road, in effect. One of those branches most likely will be the out trail, from bedding to feeding, and the other branch the in trail, from feeding back to bedding. There will be several of these, remember, because deer have more than one bedding area and more than one feeding area. I think we often want to think of only one bedding area because we live only in one house and unconsciously assign the same traits to deer. Other conditions, such as wind direction, will play a strong part in helping the deer decide which trails become which.

Most hunters set up too close to the food source, which means they will be on one of the branches of the Y system. They have a 50-50 chance to pick the right trail if they can't find tracks indicating direction of movement or if they don't do any other scouting.

There is a point where the in trails and out trails merge or almost merge, and that's where you should set up. This, again, will be closer to the bedding area than most hunters set up, and it will demand that you make your setup quietly and quickly . . . all the more reason to do your scouting and stand preparation in the spring, when you have the time and can make the noise.

All in all, it is more of a loose looping effect than two distinct trails.

Doe Trails and Buck Trails

There aren't so much doe trails as there are trails used by does, fawns and young bucks. Young bucks are still kids, still following the main groupings, wondering what's going on, trying to figure things out, feeling the juices flowing. Yeah . . . they're like a bunch of teenagers. These young bucks have things to prove. They probably think they know it all, but no one will listen, and they can't boss anyone around except maybe some does and fawns.

Mature bucks don't travel these trails much, if at all, except during rut.

Basically, as has been noted earlier but is worth repeating, they don't have distinct trails. They may parallel distinct trails, but they can be 10 yards away, 20 yards away. If the trail goes through especially thick cover, bucks might travel on it just because it is easiest. The trail might veer off the thicket, but bucks will stay somewhere in the thickest cover. You'll find them using every bit of additional cover they can.

• *Scrapes along field edges usually don't amount to much, but Fratzke has found that primary scrapes can be located here in areas that see very little human disturbance.*

Are There "Hotspots?"

My definition of a "hotspot" is that **there isn't such a thing.** There is no place where the deer are going to be coming out so thick you can wait a bit and take your pick. Deer are deer. They have basic patterns, and they take what they're given. They adapt well, and they are influenced by terrain and cover and food. When all or nearly all the conditions are good, then there will be a concentration of deer because that area can support more deer.

Or if you're looking for trophy bucks, then there will be areas which will have the right conditions to let bucks develop well, grow big antlers, have the right genetic base and live long enough to be truly mature. In my area, we get trophy bucks that are only 3½ years old. I wonder what some of them would have been like at 4½, 5½ or 6½, when they're in the peak of their maturity.

So you could call such areas "hotspots" if you want, but they're just good areas. "Hotspot" seems to imply there is some special magnet, like catnip for the house cat, which draws deer there, and that this hotspot is temporary and may disappear as quickly as it seemed to appear if you say the wrong word or think the wrong thoughts.

The only hotspots that exist, you create simply by finding the best deer habitat areas and then figuring out how best to hunt them. "Hotspot" too often means something mysterious and magical to the hunter who thinks he's found one. My only response is that he's full of deer pellets.

• The only hotspots are the ones you create. You can start creating them by checking feeding areas, then trails to bedding areas and analyzing your findings.

• *Trail threading, shown here with a light rope so the concept is easily visible, is one way to check deer directional movement when tracks don't show, and time of movement (if you check often enough).*

You still have to know how to hunt an area. Dave Morrison and I were talking about that last spring. He had just scouted over some area and said he found a place where someone else was hunting, but the guy was about 50 yards off the main action. Dave looked it all over and concluded the guy could stand there all day and never see a deer. The deer could pick him up and scoot around him.

The guy didn't do his homework. He just, apparently, got out there before the season and it was probably a corner and looked natural, he'd read all about hunting the edges, so he set up. You aren't very often going to see good bucks near the edges. Dave said this guy would have been lucky to see one in four deer which moved through the area.

That's typical of hunters. They don't scout enough to recognize the exact best location for a stand, they can't make their own hotspots.

Finding deer isn't the whole answer, either. You have to learn how to hunt them . . . in that particular area. You can't go by rules of thumb. They're too general. You have to get in and learn that area, its cover and its winds. That's just the same as fine tuning your bow.

Scouting

Are Primary Scrapes Generally Found in Thick Cover?

Yes and no, in the sense that the actual primary scrapes aren't in thick cover, but they generally are surrounded by thick cover. Once you're in the general scrape area, you'd be surprised at how much shooting area you do have, but I also think conditions that tight are all to the deer's advantage. What they don't smell or see, they can hear.

A doe standing in the general area, waiting for an acceptable buck, doesn't need to be visible to that buck. That buck does more scent checking, especially if it is a good buck, to determine whether the doe is ready to accept a buck. If your scent is mixed in there because you're too close, or you move and the buck picks it up, you've had it.

Primary scrapes in isolated areas with little or no human pressure are not always in thick cover. This happens now and then in my hunting areas. They will be along field edges or back from the edge 15 or 20 yards. They also will be near ridge saddles where deer movement from one side of the ridge to the other will be concentrated.

• *Primary scrapes don't always have to be huge. Fratzke has found that they may be relatively small in large wooded areas. If you don't check closely and often enough (to see how frequently they're freshened) you can miss them.*

Chapter 3
Preparing Yourself and Your Equipment

Scouting is part of it. Hunting is part of it. Your shooting and equipment preparation is the third part. A triangle is a very strong configuration and that's what you ought to have here.

You can prepare yourself as a target archer. You also can over-prepare yourself. You cannot use highly polished shooting skills as a hunting crutch. **Shooting skill does not substitute for scouting and hunting skills.**

I shoot an average of twice a week all summer in some sort of competitive archery. I shoot a lot of field archery. This frequency isn't a must for everyone; I just happen to like to shoot.

Carp shooting in the spring is another opportunity to sharpen actual shooting skills. That's fast shooting. You get good training on handling

• If you'll be hunting from a tree-stand, practice from that elevation. Note, below, how the angle makes your target smaller, which can make it seem further away than it is and which can cause you to shoot high.

• When an animal is quartering, remember to adjust point of impact forward or backward as necessary so your arrow's path leads through the vital area instead of ahead or behind it.

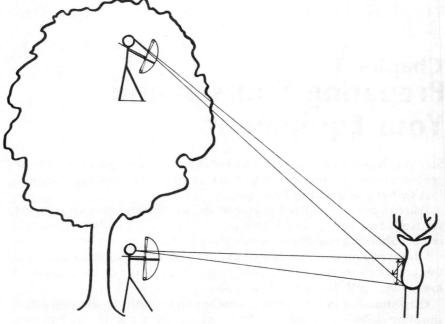

Prepare Yourself/Gear

the bow, drawing and aiming and releasing. It's a form of hunting, and the real thing is better than a practice round any time.

You need a summer to get to know the bow, to make it and your total shot a smooth machine. Tuning a bow is important. There are certain little tricks to making arrows fly better. You don't pick up those things overnight.

All this might mean is a slight nock adjustment, arrow rest adjustment, pressure point adjustment. It might even mean cranking your bow up or down in draw weight a bit to tune **it** to your arrows (less expensive than buying new arrows, and usually results in a better match). Sometimes this adjustment really makes a difference in how your arrows fly.

Note: Check your bow's listed draw weight on a scale. Once in a while one is mis-marked. We've seen guys go crazy trying to tune a bow, then discover they were trying to tune to an incorrect draw weight.

I shoot a target bow at target draw weight with target weight arrows. I'll also shoot a heavier draw weight hunting bow with hunting weight arrows. It only takes a matter of two or three arrows to convert my instinctive aiming from one to the other. This is because the arrow trajectory for each setup is roughly the same.

There's not much sense practicing on pie plates, either. There's no season on pie plates. **Shoot at targets that look like the animal you'll be shooting at.** Get your mind and muscles accustomed to the right visual setting. You can evaluate each shot to see whether you have good placement on the deer, both point of entry and path through the animal.

Broadhead tuning is essential and can be done in a special way that is no trouble. Get half a dozen extra broadheads of the type you will use for hunting. Put them on your arrows and practice with them. They'll get dinged and dull, but so what. Do you want to know where the broadhead-tipped arrows fly or don't you? They're sure going to have a different point of impact from arrows with field points.

When it is hunting time, put completely new heads on and go. You know where the arrows will hit. You have confidence. Don't take a chance on any possible dings in the ferrule or blade slots or point.

Overbowing

This is a common problem, even among archery club members, who you would think would **not** have that problem. You have to be able to handle your bow under any given situation . . . in a tree stand, in cramped or twisted conditions, in cold weather when the muscles don't work as well and reflexes are poorer.

I'm 6'1'' and weigh 225, so I'm not small. **I shoot a 63-pound bow. I can shoot that bow and get excellent penetration on any whitetail, any kind of shot I want to take at it.** Plus, I can handle that bow under any condition . . . when a deer is directly beneath me, which is a tough direction to draw and shoot, and in cold weather. Late seasons — prime hunting time — can be tough on you. The longer you stand, the colder you get, the harder it is to pull that bow back. The harder it is to pull it back, the less accurate you're going to be. Those are some big negatives regarding too much bow draw weight.

There's just no question about it. Don't overbow yourself. **It's better to be more accurate than to be shooting a heavier draw weight.**

The fact that you know you can handle your bow under **all** shooting conditions gives you confidence in your shooting ability, plus added confidence in the field.

Confidence in the field is probably one of the major factors in this whole business of hunting . . . your confidence in yourself, in your scouting results, in your hunting ability. You built that confidence, you didn't just go out and buy it. You built it from the ground up. You picked your tree stand sites. You set up and tuned your bow and got it humming. You took care to make sure you did everything right, did them the best you could.

I repeat — this confidence factor is probably the biggest of all. Without it, you aren't going to be able to sit quietly and comfortably for long hours. I really believe that a person without confidence acts wrong, often impulsively, and almost radiates that lack of confidence.

You can't go out there and second-guess yourself all the time. Sure, you can admit mistakes — you have to admit mistakes or else you're just kidding yourself. You can learn from them.

That's why I say that whitetail deer aren't a magical being. They aren't mysterious. They are highly developed and well adapted to their niche in life. There just are a lot of things that we don't know about them yet, haven't learned about them. Assigning them a semi-godlike nature only slows down our learning process. I give the whitetail a lot of credit, but I can't give it that much credit.

Don't beat yourself!

Use your common sense. Don't over-think. Try to use your instincts. These conditions, developed right, will make you a better hunter and sportsman. Hunt and scout as often as possible. With experience, you will gain much more knowledge and confidence. You just never stop learning. Common sense tells you that the more you're out there, the better you will know the prey you're hunting . . . if you have an open mind, think, analyze and see what you're looking at. Do what the deer does — take what you're given and make it work.

Why I use my Particular Shooting Style

I like a high anchor and I like gun-barreling. That gives me a much better line of sight on that deer at 20 to 25 yards. I don't like to shoot any more at longer distances. Too many chances for marginal hits. Too many chances

• *You can improve your overall hunting and shooting skills by attending bowhunting seminars and participating in field and broadhead shoots. In addition, you'll pick up hunting and shooting tips from other people, which ought to help you avoid making every mistake yourself, thus shortening the time necessary to advance your skills.*

to pick the wrong sight pin. Too many chances to misjudge the distance, and with an arrow even a couple of yards off is critical. I'd rather work on my scouting and hunting abilities and get so I can set up in a place and at a distance which will give me a good shot at the right distance at a deer that doesn't know I'm there. That takes a lot of the guesswork out of it.

Edge hunting is tempting, because you see plenty of deer. However, we tend to overlook the fact that almost all of those deer are out of good shot range or are grossly out of good shot range.

Prepare Yourself/Gear   51

That's why I set up to do most of my shooting at 20-25 yards — back in the thicker areas where fewer deer are seen but they are better deer.

Just like on the big one I missed in 1981. I've taken a lot of animals with a head-on shot, sticking the arrow in at the base of the neck and running it down through the heart. That, however, is chancey. There's only about a two-inch circle at the base of the neck for an ideal target. The rest is surrounded and covered by bone and muscle. It's not that good a shot from a tree stand.

A straight down shot isn't much, either. Too much bone and muscle protection, not enough chance for full penetration. A deer hit high without full penetration can run a long way before it spills a drop of blood and could too easily be a lost deer.

This all is a personal choice. **Your shooting and aiming style must be a personal choice, whatever works best for you, is most comfortable and gives you the most confidence.** I've given you the reasons I prefer my style; if they help you decide, fine. If not, remember that it's all trial and error and personal choice.

Equipment Setup

Keep it simple. Do everything you can just to be quiet . . . on clothes, stand, bow and attachments.

A bow quiver is a prime example. Just from your walking through the woods, arrows can work loose. When you climb into your stand, check the arrows. Push them up firmly into the hood against the soft lining or holder. Loose arrows cause a lot of vibration when you're shooting, maybe enough to make the deer jump. A quiver on the side of a bow is a form of a stabilizer, so if it and everything in it are vibrating like crazy, who knows what could happen?

Check your bow. Give the bowstring a strum. It will tell you whether anything is loose.

By now, I think the need for camouflage and silencers has been pretty well explained.

A good hunting arrow rest is important. It also gets much less attention than it should. A good arrow rest will work under all conditions. It **has** to work under all conditions. Don't go with plastics that are too flimsy and weak or springs that are noisy. If you have an arrow rest with a plain spring, cover that with moleskin or something similar . . . a piece of tape if you have nothing else. I think deer often jump the sound of the arrow being drawn across the rest instead of jumping the string. **The necessity of having the arrow rest quiet is one of the biggest factors in the whole setup.**

Use an arrow holder. Your fingers can get tired of holding the arrow in place; your finger will apply too much pressure on the arrow and thus the

• *Silence is extremely important, and the arrow rest and area around it are one of the critical spots. Use moleskin or similar adhesive material here. Teflon on the cable guard reduces friction, which can help bow performance. Warm mitts that also permit good string control are ideal for cold weather. If you're cold, you don't hunt or shoot as well. In bowhunting, attention to details is essential.*

arrow rest; when you hang your bow on a tree branch or whatever, you want the arrow to stay in place when you pick up that bow again to draw on a deer. **Be sure the arrow holder slot fits the arrow right.** If it's too tight, the arrow can be pulled right off the string as you draw.

I use only feather fletching, because feathers are the most forgiveable and provide the most control. I put Scotch-Guard on them for damp weather, and then I make sure they're dried right away when I come in out of damp weather. If it begins to rain, I have them covered with a hood. A feather can be noisy if brushed against, but there are few chances of that, and my camo clothing is soft, so that minimizes the chance.

I like bright fletching on my number one arrow. I want to see where my arrow hits the deer, and the brightness is helpful in following the deer if the fletching doesn't go into or through the deer. It's also easier to find such an arrow after it has gone through a deer. Some people figure the brightness scares deer; it won't if you are in the right position and move right.

I use a bright nock, for the same reason. A little bit of reflective tape under the nock, on the swedging, really glistens. It doesn't affect the glueing, either.

The rest of the arrow I try to keep toned down a bit, especially my backup arrows which I might need to shoot when the animal is a bit alarmed.

I find that most quivers, in order to make them work best, need some kind of adjustment, either to get the feathers angled back so they won't get messed up when brush hits them or for best hanging in a tree.

I've never liked peep sights, because they can be difficult to use and slow you down more than you want. Nine times out of ten, you're going to be shooting under poor light conditions. If you're shooting with a headnet, this can complicate it. Remember that shooting through netting affects depth perception a bit, so practice with one if you intend to hunt that way.

Remember to practice from the stand height if you'll hunt from a stand. Practice in low light conditions too, so you'll be familiar with those visual conditions. **Low light conditions affect depth perception a lot, so if you haven't practiced under those conditions you can blow a good situation.**

• *Quivers can be noisy and glare in the light. Cover them and be sure all attachments are tight. Check your arrows, too, for firm seating in the clips and in the hood.*

Prepare Yourself/Goal

• Binoculars are an important accessory, even in heavy cover. From your stand, you can check quite a bit of area without leaving scent, check individual animals and help identify hit location after the shot.

• A lined pouch hanging from your belt will keep your bowhand warm in cold weather. It also is a good place to stash small accessories.

Prepare Yourself/Goal

My field pack is designed for one thing — to store hunting clothes. When I'm going to my treestand I dress for walking, not standing. The extra clothes go in the pack and I put them on after I cool off on the stand. The pack also has tree steps, buck lure during the rut, cotton balls in cannisters, small first aid kit, folding pocket saw, and that's about it. Plus the surgeon's gloves for my allergy. I don't carry a bunch of tools or other things. My plans are to hunt, not open a repair shop. On stand, I tie the pack to the other side of the tree with its own straps.

Binoculars are important. Use the best pair you can afford. They are a tool of the trade. I use 7x24 mini-binoculars when I'm scouting and hunting. They can cover a lot of ground faster than my feet can. I like to get a good look at animals, too; on overcast days antlers don't show up very well, so binoculars then help. I also use them to determine what type of animal is in my stand area, maybe one I missed with my scouting.

Does Bob Fratzke miss any shots?

That's a good one. And thank you for the compliment. The buck I missed in 1981 was the biggest buck, in antler score, I've ever shot at. Ten yards away. He was moving before I released. I think his sixth sense did something. He was too close to me, and it was an absolutely calm morning. He came in head-on, and I had to wait. All the shots would have been head-on, and I couldn't have been sure enough. I still can't believe I missed. I'd rather have that, however, than a poor head-on shot which might have killed him but could just as easily have left too poor a trail to follow for recovery of the animal.

I got the dry heaves after that buck so bad I thought I was going to fall out of my tree.

I've missed a lot more than I've taken. It wasn't buck fever; I think it was more target panic. It was knowing that I had the animal dead to rights. I just couldn't deliver the shot at the right time. I flinched or didn't have something under control. That was **not** mind over matter, which it should have been and which can be learned. I got so disgusted with myself a few times I almost quit hunting.

Almost . . . but not quite.

I hung up on those shots, in that I couldn't release the string. I was changing my mind when I should have been acting.

You have to get so you can act and react instead of think at the moment of truth. If you have to think about it or have the slightest hesitation, there's a good chance you'll miss. When you bring the bow up, you must have a feeling all the way through you. When you do, that arrow is gone before you realize it. Your knowledge and training take charge.

• A daypack can carry enough items to open an archery shop, but it needs to carry extra clothes and the few essentials. Lower right, camouflage the bottom of your treestand with spray paint and a stencil of different patterns. Below, push-pins with reflective tape can be stuck on the side of the tree so you can use them for references in your flashlight beam entering or leaving the woods.

• In tight situations, example above, you'll need to go higher in the tree so deer will be less likely to catch your movement and so your scent will be less likely to give you away. Water is more of a barrier, left photo, to us than to deer. If you get back in the swamps, you ought to find a better buck:doe ratio and fewer hunters.

Chapter 4
Hunting Season

During the Season — Scout more than Hunt

I scout more than I hunt during the hunting season. For two reasons: 1) I can do it because I know where I want to be when I set up, 2) I have a pretty good idea where the deer are going to be. This means that I can make most efficient use of my hunting time. This is possible because I have many stand locations in scattered areas. They all need checking to see which is or are best at certain times. Then I hunt the ones I select.

For instance, there will be areas I have scouted as likely candidates for primary breeding areas. As the rut approaches, I'll keep checking them and evaluating them, see whether deer are using them with the same pattern of use as the previous year. Then I'll set up my hunting according to what the signs and previous experience tell me.

As I have said before, 90 percent of my time in the woods (during a year) is spent scouting. **Only 10 percent of my total time is spent actually hunting.**

I'll take an afternoon off (rather than a morning, because I prefer to hunt mornings) and go scout an area I plan to hunt the next week. This is where hunters often foul up — they scout the area they're hunting in right now, which messes it up. Disturbance must be kept to a minimum.

I'm looking for all signs, of course, but principally rubs. Rubs will be found in relationship to deer trails and their normal movement patterns. If I find a line of them, I can use that line to get a lead on where the buck or bucks may have been coming from and heading toward, if I don't already know it. In my areas, rubs are either just off the ridge top or down near the bottom right off the field.

Rubs are a good indication of the body size of the deer and of the antler size. You know that a six-inch popple deeply gouged had one hell of a buck leaning on it at one time. Big deer won't rub big trees exclusively, but you know that when a big tree is rubbed, it was done by a big deer.

I don't believe rubs mark territories. Territories aren't quite that well defined. **Rubs simply occur in a location that is well suited to the buck on his normal movement patterns.** Bucks rub in these areas year after year if their travel patterns are the same. So if you find rubs in a previously unused area, you have an indication of some change in buck movement which will bear further checking to determine the details.

• *This one, taken a few years ago, brings the right type of smile. It just missed Pope and Young minimum of 125 points.*

One thing I've noticed the past couple of years in my area: Bucks seem to be rubbing less than they did. I'm seeing more deer and better deer, but the rubs just aren't there. I don't know if they're losing that characteristic or what. Maybe rubbing is an aggression outlet and something has happened to take the place of rubbing. Seems to differ from buck to buck, so maybe it is a genetic thing which varies with the individual. I've talked with other good bowhunters in this area, and they have noticed it too. Maybe it has something to do with the age ratio in a herd. We have more good bucks now than we've ever had, which would seem to tell me that we have a more mature herd.

Getting back to other scouting in hunting season, there's the usual list you can't overlook — checking trails for fresh use, checking with thread or tracks to see direction of movement, examining pellets to see what deer are eating. Check the food sources, to see if and where and when they are being used. On deer pellets, you can tell if a deer if still feeding heavily on alfalfa or other lush grazing foods because the pellets aren't really pellets. The scat is softer and usually in one lump, looking much like sheep droppings.

Early Season Hunting

I mentioned earlier that I generally hunt an area for good bucks, instead of hunting a specific good buck. In an instance like I just mentioned, where I have one pretty well programmed, I'll go after him specifically. Common sense tells me that a) I'm only going to have so much time in the woods before or after work, and b) I'm only going to have, probably, one good chance at that dude. So as long as I have him patterned, there's not much sense passing him up.

If I fail to get that particular buck, I go back to generalizing my hunting as the season goes on. Those bucks don't have big walls around their territories. Territories overlap, so movement overlaps. Sometimes a little, sometimes a lot. **More during rut — the bucks' area doubles or triples during rut, while the does' area stays about the same, but they move more through it. The further deer have to go between feeding and bedding, the more overlap there is and the more chances you have because the more exposed the deer will be.** Then it becomes percentage hunting, you figuring where the best spot is to catch deer moving through a given good area.

Summer movement patterns will carry over into the first week of season only, sometimes the first weekend only. After that, the deer are reacting to stress again. The only good time you're going to have a chance at trophy bucks outside the rut is the first day or two of the season.

A friend of mine, a good hunter, says that if he can't get a buck in the first two weeks of season, he almost feels like quitting hunting until rut. This is a little extreme, but it is basically true if you're looking for big

• *Shank Scharmach with his 1981 buck. It scored 138-3/8. Note the size of its neck.*

bucks. Sightings will drop way off. The big ones will travel mainly at night and they won't travel any more than they have to. This means that if you're going to go in after them, you have a good chance of setting up too close to their bedding areas and quite possibly spooking them. You don't want to do that, because spooking deer out of their bedding areas can goof up the hunting for a long time.

You want those deer to feel they have a sanctuary. The bedding area is that sanctuary.

Another important factor in October is that acorns drop. Deer can feed on them, fill up on them actually, without getting out of the woods or hardly exposing themselves — unless you know where the good oaks are and position yourself there. Deer practically take up residence in a good white oak area when acorns fall.

Those conditions, plus the increased human traffic in the woods, make it perfectly understandable why there isn't much trophy buck action until the rut gets going. The thing which helps here is that bucks pick up their action before the does are ready to breed.

You will find false scrapes and little starter scrapes along fencerows and in other places of normal movement. Most of these seem to be made simply because the bucks were beginning to feel the urge.

The Effect of Stress . . . Improved Morning Hunting

Deer move differently under the effects of stress. I'm talking of the stress produced by people in the woods — squirrel hunters, bird hunters, hikers, bowhunters scouting like last-minute Christmas shoppers, etc. **Stress is the one condition which seems to bother deer the most and changes their patterns the most, for the obvious reason.** Human activity is the prime interruption of their standard patterns.

They begin doing more of their travelling at night, which is why morning hunting becomes better. Deer feed and bed down intermittently all night, becoming more relaxed because there's been little or no human traffic for several hours.

The toughest part of morning hunting is getting out of bed. As the weather gets colder, this involves serious talking to yourself now and then. The thing which ought to keep you going is that with morning hunting you can have your best results, over the long term.

It's a mistake to believe that deer feed in one particular spot all night. They move all over. They will bed down at night right where they are feeding; that's why you can often see them in alfalfa fields.

Much of the time, though, more deer will be back along the edges, bedded down there. They're going to move to feed some more, and that probably will be in the general direction of their bedding area. There's a lot of wandering.

Morning hunting early in the season is the toughest. There's more vegetation to stumble through, more opportunity to make noises. **As the season advances it gets easier to morning hunt.** Leaves are down and traveling through the brush is easier. You can see a little more right near you and avoid some of the potential problems. If you move right, footsteps in the leaves won't be a problem. Besides, if you're clean and have rubber boots on, you can walk in deer trails to help hold down noise. They will generally have less brush, and the leaves will have been matted or chopped a bit by deer hooves. The ground is packed harder, too.

A lot of hunters don't hunt the morning right. First, they go out too late — I emphasize continually that it is better to be an hour early than a minute late — and have difficulty getting set up between deer and the bedding areas those deer are moving back to. **Silence is an important factor now, more important than usual, because generally you're working in tighter quarters.**

If you have a sand road, driveway, grassy path or anything like that which you can walk on silently, that's the right start. Your scouting will have shown you several potential stand sites on crossings in such areas. If you can get someone to drive past your stand slowly and let you hop out and get into your stand immediately, that is good. The vehicle doesn't stop, and it distracts any animals in the area.

Most hunters also don't sit long enough. They'll sit for an hour, a couple of hours, then go home. This is especially true when the weather turns cold.

Deer have a tendency to bed down shortly after sunrise. Then they get up again and feed a little in mid-morning.

Bucks are always the first ones back to the bedding area. They usually start back before daylight, maybe loafing and feeding along the way, maybe bedding down at some halfway point, maybe just wandering slowly. At this time, they generally move **into the wind,** so they know what's ahead of them and the does and other deer behind them cover their rear.

You may move deer out ahead of you as you move in. You obviously want to avoid this, but it happens. This is another reason it is best to be an hour early than a minute late. The area needs a chance to cool down. Since a deer really spooked from an area can leave a scent which alarms other deer coming through later, I believe that it is always best to move at a slow, steady pace as quietly as possible. Deer may or may not know what you are, and there's less chance they will spook under those conditions. Again, if they are the sitting instead of the running kind, you may be able to turn that good defense mechanism against them, unless you set up within their immediate zone of hearing, sight or smell.

I and the people I hunt with seem to take most of our deer from 8:30 a.m. to 11 a.m. or thereabouts. This pattern exists all during the season and is strongest during the rut. I think a certain amount of this has to do with the movement of other hunters leaving the woods. This isn't a large factor during most bowhunting situations because there aren't that many people in the woods. It is, however, a prime example of the reason you should silently and carefully move away from your morning stand when you leave, if you're in brush or other cover. The best advice I can give regarding that is to stillhunt your way out of the area.

Remember, too, that around 8:30 a.m. is when a lot of small game and bird hunters get going, especially on weekends. (They should have been out before daylight, too, because from what we've seen, gray squirrels and grouse are active at dawn, moreso than during the remainder of the day. Which fact, I think, ought to be a good indicator about the movement of most other wild animals.)

Around 8 or 8:30 a.m., there also seems to be a movement of does and fawns, and some small bucks, back to the main bedding areas. This is the only deer movement most hunters see in the morning.

The problem most hunters run into is that they can't stand long enough. If they get out before daylight, they run out of patience or dedication or whatever around 7:30 or 8 a.m. If you can't get out early and sit all morning, you may want to try going in at daybreak and sitting until 11 a.m. or so. In some conditions, this may be the best way by far, simply because you'll be able to get in much more quietly.

I generally can avoid this problem because I take my time, which gives my eyes a chance to adjust well to the almost-dark conditions. You ought to be able to have some sense as to where you're stepping and walking, when there's brush or saplings in front of you. I carry my treestand on my back most of the time like a backpack, which leaves one hand free to move that interference out of my path. Also, you'll quickly find out just how quiet or noisy your camo clothing is under these conditions. The softer it is, the better. Reflective push pins can mark a trail easily; the flashlight won't spook deer.

• *When you're looking at deer, be that in the field, at a game farm, at a zoo or wherever, note how it moves. Note how the shadows make it appear a bit further away than it is; low light conditions hinder good distance judging. Practice, mentally, picking a spot. Tell yourself when you would or would not release as the animal moves. Enjoyable practice.*

From what I've seen — and I've seen it several times — good bucks will try to bed down just like any deer right after daylight and then pick up again in the morning. They'll feed for a couple of hours in mid-morning to mid-day. They won't move as far as at dusk and dawn. They won't have to, because they feed fairly lightly. This means they can get what they want pretty close to their bedding area. Their bedding and feeding clock seems to be on about a four-hour cycle.

I've watched does and fawns bed down at various times within sight of my treestand and stay there a couple of hours. They would chew their

• *You can't be too cautious approaching a downed buck; it may not yet be dead. Approach from the rear or back so you're away from hooves and antlers. Poke it with a stick or your arrow to see if there's response.*

cud for two hours, then get up and feed. This was in a halfway area between major feeding and bedding areas.

We've been talking about stress during the day and late afternoon hunting hours improving morning hunting because deer are more relaxed and there are far fewer people in the woods.

You can, however, **put the squeeze on them and also learn quite a bit.** That's when the deer go back to old reliable, their preferred maneuvers and routes.

If I have a situation where I know a buck is going to move through, I move in on him and see what he does, where he goes. This obviously works best when there's snow on the ground for easiest tracking. Sometimes it is the only way this can be done.

Sometimes other hunters inadvertently put the squeeze on them, and I'll take up the trail and see what happens, where it went and why, if I can figure it out.

I should amend this to say "where deer do *or don't* go." Not only will deer evade a certain area if the hunting or other people pressure gets too heavy, I've seen plenty of areas where hunters took the easiest route through an area and the deer just sidestepped them. When this happens, and there's a good chance that more hunters will be through, I like to set up at what I judge will be the best spot and then let the next hunters through the area put the squeeze on the deer without the hunters even knowing it (which is what happens a lot of times to ourselves, and we don't even know deer were in the area). This is similar to scouting during the firearm season.

Evening hunting

The easiest to do. It's easier to get in front of deer moving out to feed than to get in front of deer moving back into bedding cover.

That's one reason. Another reason evening hunting is generally better for most hunters is that they can devote more time to it. Sometimes this is just an alibi because they don't want to get up early enough for morning hunting, but usually it isn't.

Evening hunting then is going to look better in the books because that's the bulk of the time spent out there by the bulk of the hunters. That simply translates into more success. On a per-hour basis, it shouldn't be that way.

A point to remember about evening hunting — the deer will be more nervous. Bucks move later, with does in front of them and wind at their back — remember, you set up **downwind** of the trails and expect to see deer come into your area. This tells us that deer, especially bucks, move with the wind more than we realize.

First Time Stands

Both of us involved in creating this book have noticed several times that there's a "first time charm" with many stands, which is all the more reason to have several well scouted stands. Several so you can keep them all relatively fresh, and well scouted so you're ready to handle any situation the first (and possibly only) time it occurs.

One of the most important reasons bowhunters often have trouble seeing deer is that their efforts are too concentrated. Lots of people misinterpret the "have plenty of stands" instruction.

I don't mean 40 stands in a 40 acre patch. You're in there, you have messed around in the area extensively, and you probably have a buddy or two hunting there. That's too much activity. Don't put all your beans in one pot. The thing to do is to find more hunting land . . . it's there if you ask for it right. Spread out your activities to avoid disturbance as much as possible; avoid creating stress in the deer.

This, then, gives you much better opportunities to have the "first time stand" situation.

There's the element of surprise in your favor. You cleaned out the stand and the shooting lanes long ago, so there's no scent hanging around and no recent vegetative change. Sometimes this first time charm occurs just as easily when you make a stand at mid-day, let it cool a few hours, then come back that evening to hunt it. Either way, it is still a fresh area. You haven't tracked up the area. You haven't scuffed up leaves setting out a scent bottle. The deer has no prior experience of stress in this particular area. **If you don't over-use an area, you can essentially hunt it fresh each time.**

The longer you sit in an area, on consecutive hunting opportunities, the *higher* the odds on not seeing deer, as far as I'm concerned. A lot of hunters figure the reverse, since a deer *has* to pass there sooner or later. Well, a deer doesn't *have* to do anything except eat, move, hide and reproduce. There are plenty of other areas for all of that.

Hunting the Rut

If you're going to take vacation time to hunt — or even if you're not — this is the time to be in the woods.

Since most states go off daylight saving time about that time or just before it, I've found that hunting pressure actually drops in most areas at this time. By the time you get home from work, clean up, get ready, then get out there, it's dark. Too late. This generally leaves the weekend for most people.

So if you've been in the woods all day during the week, you have great hunting with generally less hunting pressure. That's an excellent combination. Since there are fewer daylight hours then, too, you can stand all day much easier than you could earlier in the season.

Hunt the Does

Does have familiar patterns. They are much more predictable than bucks. They generally run trails, good trails. They basically make the trails . . . they, yearlings and young bucks . . . from bedding to feeding areas and back.

Bucks will be looking for them, so it is common sense to figure that scrapes will appear in good areas where does will be moving through but which bucks can check without exposing themselves. **Scrapes become the community bulletin board, not the main breeding areas.**

The key is to look for a network of trails. Does will have the main, noticeable network. Bucks will have their own looser network, tougher to find, tougher to see and not particularly aligned with the does network but possibly at crossing directions. They like shortcuts. They also prefer to feed at night.

They aren't lazier, just more cautious. More naturally cautious I believe, but you'll also notice that when does are hunted regularly it doesn't take long for them to adapt either. I believe bucks know their main purpose is for breeding only.

Scrapes and Scrape Hunting

The rut in my area starts the last week in October, but there's a false rut before that. This false rut shows up in mid-September. You'll find scrapes around the edge of fields, sometimes under an overhanging branch, sometimes not. If there is a branch, usually it is an oak branch. The tip of the branch may be chewed off, but don't depend on it.

Basically, bucks then are just going through the motions. This is when the first bit of the male hormone called testosterone must start flowing.

You can shoot bucks off these scrapes, but this is due more to the fact that these scrapes show up along their normal travel routes than because they're doing any checking. The buck happened to be there and felt like pawing, as opposed to going to a primary breeding area, which doesn't yet exist.

False rut scrapes are the least meaningful, for the reasons given.

Secondary scrapes can be as good as the primary scrape because they're all made in the same general area, and they all start out as secondary scrapes. The key here is "area." The first doe in heat, I believe, decides which scrape will be the primary scrape by coming into that area and urinating in one of them. This draws the bucks' attentions, and the checking, urinating and entire breeding process increases activity on that particular scrape, but also for the others in the area.

Here you have a wheel effect, with the primary scrape as the hub. Does coming to it will hit the secondary scrapes first, probably, and possibly stop at one of them a while. Since the trophy buck will be scent checking the scrapes from outside and downwind of the general area, he's often just as likely to pick up the scent of a doe at a secondary scrape. If she's ready, he'll know it, and the secondary scrape has served its purpose as well as a primary scrape could.

The primary scrape is still the key, however, because when it is opened up, they all improve. I think that's simple common sense. Until the primary is begun, however, they will be of equal value. I repeat: All scrapes in that good **area** are secondary until the primary is created.

Good scrapes aren't always in open areas in thick cover. I know of several big scrapes on the edges of fields or near the edges in areas where not much human activity occurs. These can be, and are, primary scrapes. I've noticed they always occur at some halfway point on a ridge or other edge where there's a saddle, or other semi-protected area for deer to go over the top of the ridge rather than go all the way around the ridge in brushy cover. Again . . . primary **scrapes occur where there is good, natural deer movement.**

I've also found that **larger (six to seven feet square) scrapes generally occur in smaller woodlots instead of big woods.** I believe this is because deer have more area to travel and hide in in a big woods, so there are more places where scraping areas and breeding areas can occur. However, in a small area, such as a woodlot, all the deer must travel through this more-restricted cover, so there are fewer places for good scrape areas to develop, and those which do develop will see tremendous activity.

Note that I said **primary scrapes in larger woods don't need to be very large.** If you've been judging the scrape's importance by its size in such areas, you may have been missing a key signal or signals.

I don't pay much attention to when scrapes may have been made or the direction the dirt was thrown. Ninety percent of the scrape making in

this area is at night. Some will be in late afternoon and early evening, but this is mainly by smaller bucks working off some of their randiness. With the types of circular routes we generally have, either true circular or of the hour-glass nature, and with the interruptions their traveling can have, if you set up right you have a decent chance if the buck passes at the time you're there. Good bucks just don't maintain a clockwork travel pattern, so the irregularity throws some of this attempted predictability out the window.

Bucks are ready to breed a couple of weeks before does are receptive, so you can start buck hunting on scrape lines and wheels before the deer all go crazy. But, as always, you need to do it carefully, more carefully than during the rut if only because there's less activity then and the bucks won't be as likely to be moving much out of their non-rut patterns.

The bucks will be looking for does, naturally, but without luck. Young bucks may respond well now to sex lure scents. Trophy bucks aren't going to be on the prod that much yet. They're dominant, and all the bucks generally know it . . . but it will need to be re-proven. Since big bucks are always less active, more deliberate and cautious in their movement, it almost seems like they don't want to waste their energy until absolutely necessary. When it's time to get serious, they'll get serious.

The younger, smaller bucks are going to act like the second-fiddle players they basically are. They don't have a turf they can call their own. During the summer they will run with larger bucks as well as bucks their own size. They learn then which bucks are stronger and which aren't, just like the pecking order in chickens or a barnyard of cows working out which is boss at the feeder.

When the testosterone levels begin rising, these young bucks get in a hurry. They end up doing some of the breeding — or all of it in areas where the deer are cropped so heavily no bucks can mature to trophy size. These younger bucks are persistent and outnumber the bigger bucks. A big buck can't keep them all away from does in heat and doesn't try. The bucks don't form harems.

As the rut begins, the big bucks definitely will be loners. They'll start moving and go crazy when the does begin opening primary scrapes. The competitiveness asserts itself and dominance is re-proven.

Set-Up Area

You can call it the primary scrape area, the breeding area, the set-up area. I call it the set-up area; it is the **area of primary scrape and secondary scrapes which I evaluate so I can place my tree stand locations exactly as I want them.**

Once the doe comes to the primary scrape and urinates in it and on the inside of her hocks, she's marked it and will be leaving a nice trail. I don't believe it's all that important for her to hang that close to the scrape. A buck will find her.

I've seen does stand around 15 to 20 minutes after marking a scrape. I've also seen them leave almost immediately. They won't travel far, though, while they wait.

The main thing for a set-up area is that it has to be in an area with good deer travel, where they cross a lot, usually with several trails coming through the general area. This helps form the wheel and hub effect.

Scrape Checking

The bigger bucks usually hang back and scent check the scrape. The only time I've seen a big buck go right through a scrape is when he is following a doe that is right at peak of estrus. He didn't know or care where he was in relation to terrain or scrape; he had one thing on his mind and would have followed that doe through a brick wall.

You need to **set up on the downwind side of whatever trail or trails the dominant bucks will use to scent check the scrapes,** however far these trails may be from the actual scrape. This could be as far as 75 or 100 yards; only good scouting and plenty of time in the woods during rut will prove the area for you.

The smaller bucks are more likely to come in to the scrape and hang around. They probably will be there early or more frequently (or more frequently visible) because if they're going to get in on the fun they have to be in a hurry. The dominant bucks will run them off as soon as they can.

If you're more interested in shooting any buck, I'd say you ought to set up fairly close to the scrape, somewhere which will have you downwind of most of the trails coming into that hub area. Since bucks generally, but not always, approach scrapes from the same direction (because of wind direction and their general movement pattern), this factor can be of some help in your stand location decision.

Now . . . here's something I've noticed regarding trail checking by bucks. **They will cross-check trails coming into scrapes.** They will cross-check all trails, actually.

By this, I mean that I've seen lots of bucks — enough to convince me it is a pattern and not accidental behavior — moving at right angles to the doe trails. They can check all the trails, and thus, theoretically, all the does, with a minimum of movement while staying relatively close to the hubs of the scraping areas. They can go from one good scraping area to another, make their loop check, maybe taking in the secondary as well as primary scrapes, then go to the next scraping area and do the same.

Since primary scrape areas occur in openings in heavy cover, they can do all their checking with minimal exposure. They won't even be that heavily exposed when checking secondary scrapes.

Not a bad deal for them, huh?

I usually see the moving in stop-and-go fashion in these areas. The doe comes in, the buck is 50 yards or so behind her. The doe stops, the buck stops. The doe moves, the buck moves. If the doe is ready to accept that buck, they will move back into the brush away from the scrape to breed, and you won't see that buck for a day or so unless you see the doe again first. He just won't move unless she moves.

With that cross-trailing buck, you might or might not get a shot at him. He's picking up and evaluating scents. But since you have no control over where the does are or move, this is why you have to hunt doe trails if you can't hunt scrape areas. Trails generally get the most action because there's more deer passing through.

On the cross-checking of trails, I've found that it occurs most frequently when there are bucks in competition with each other.

Here's the thing to remember. You get a doe coming in, and you can tell if there's a buck hanging back. She will have a tendency to stop and look back over her shoulder. She also has a fast, nervous walk or is running hard if she isn't ready to be bred.

Whatever that doe does, that determines what the buck is going to do. If she gets spooky and starts to take off, you just keep your eye on the doe first. The buck . . . he doesn't know what's coming off. He's just following the doe. He has only one thing on his mind. So you watch her, then

• Fratzke and a 1972 whitetail of respectable dimensions.

him. What she does will help you decide when to shoot at him.

Bucks key off the does so completely that they will follow them right on into the feeding area.

Moon Phases & Sex Lure Placement

These two items are not interwoven. We placed them together simply because the example we're relating here involved both of them and is sort of a classical "how it ought to work" situation.

You're going to have probably only two or three full moons during the season, and a one-month season will have only one full moon unless it begins and ends on a full moon. Most people believe that deer travel later at night then, but they travel late at night all the time. So there really isn't that much difference; not in my area, at least. If your scouting and hunting shows a definite difference from my findings, go with what your findings tell you. Deer vary from region to region, and it's what's happening in your hunting area which counts.

The thing is . . . if you're set up where you should be set up, you're going to be back in the cover somewhere. At other times, you'll be seeing deer movement reasonably early in the afternoon, now during a full moon you may not see it as early, but you still ought to see deer during shooting hours. I haven't noticed a full moon affecting deer movement much one way or the other. Weather can have more effect.

During the rut, with all the deer movement, that reproductive urge has more effect than a deer's looking in the sky, noting a full moon and deciding to move later because it will be little darker then.

Last year during the rut, I shot a good buck an hour before legal closing time. The moon was full. I had enough time left to follow the deer and field dress him. I thought I'd pick him up the next morning, so I took off my tee-shirt and hung it on his body to keep coyotes off. (Yes, we have a few coyotes in our area, and we're getting more.)

After dinner, we decided to get the buck, so we wouldn't screw up the morning hunting for the other fellows in the party. It would be a long drag, all the way from the valley up to the top.

As I was parking the truck, here came a nice buck chasing a doe right across the ridgetop field. He came out right where I had shot the buck, so he and the does had to have run right past the buck's carcass. Didn't bother them at all.

This was at 9 p.m. The full moon was high and bright. We didn't have any trouble getting the buck out because we could see where we were walking. It was almost like broad daylight.

The buck was taken the last of October in Minnesota. **He came right to my buck lure on an extremely quiet day, not my favorite hunting condition.** There was just enough breeze blowing across the ridgetop to keep the area clean of my scent and distribute the sex scent well.

The buck would have missed me by 100 yards ordinarily. I was standing in a tree, facing north with the wind out of the northwest. The lure was 15 yards to my right and a little bit in front of me.

Deer funnelling from the northwest, north or northeast to the south, I'd see as they approached. My stand was sort of right at the base of the funnel. Bucks don't always travel the doe trails during the rut because they're ready before the does (this was late October, remember, and the bucks were ready but the does weren't).

I had set the scent out to cover the entire ridge area behind me. There was a good chance deer would be moving east to west in that area, so with the sex lure on my right, east of me, any buck moving from the east would pick up the lure scent before it would have a chance to pick up my scent.

You always want to place attractant lures in such a way that your scent and the lure scent blow parallel and as far apart as is practical, for reasons which I think are obvious. Any time your scent and the deer lure scent are mixed, that gives strange signals to any deer which may have been attracted. If you pour out a whole dose of deer lure, hoping that it will overpower your scent, you've shot yourself down. **In the use of scents, any scents, too little is better than too much. This is the reverse of camouflage. You never can have too much camouflage, but you certainly can have too much scent in use.**

Since I was on the north side of a tree, any deer coming in from behind me would have its attention riveted on the lure, and I'd be out of its sight. Also, when it would come within the right angle to possibly pick up my scent, it couldn't because my scent would be blowing above it. So, in effect, I really was hunting the full circle of cover around me. Since I was on a ridgetop, my scent was drifting out off the top of the ridge a good distance before cooling and sinking down. The lure scent, however, being only about 15 inches above the ground, was following the ground surface breezes.

Basically, what happens, or should happen, when you set up such a lure is that the deer will come from the directions you don't expect them. You always position yourself downwind of the principle area you're hunting, for the obvious scent-hiding reasons, which means that sex lure scent **cannot** be upwind straight in front of you if it is to do any good. **The scent hunts the area behind you** *always*, **if you're set up right.**

So any deer moving past behind you, whether it came in from way behind you or whether it came in from either side, or whether it moved down from the direction in front of you but too far to the side . . . they all stand a chance of hitting that scent line and following it in. Those which move in from in front of you but too far to the side may have to circle to find it, and there's obviously no guarantee that will happen, not even when the trail crosses the scent line or they just decide to go that direction.

Because of all this, there's a better than even chance that with a sex lure scent during the early rut and the full rut, you're going to be bringing in more deer from the direction you didn't expect and/or are least able to cover. But since you want to place that lure a bit ahead of you as well as to the side, any deer coming to the lure should give you a nice, quartering shot as it moves to the lure. This means you have to watch behind you as well as in front.

The cotton ball had three drops of scent. That's all. Fresh drops on a clean ball. I use a new cotton ball with three drops of fresh scent each time I go out. The cotton ball is stuck on a twig. When I leave, I put the cotton ball in a 35mm plastic film cannister, take it out of the woods and throw it in the garbage.

The buck came in like he was on a string. I couldn't believe he was coming in. He made a half circle to the east and north, so he actually approached the cotton ball from upwind. I don't know whether that's significant or not, because the half-circle was made close to the cotton ball. I think it was more like you'll see a dog or cat circle something when it is close, just sort of to size it up from all angles.

He stopped once, then came in all stretched out until his nose was about a foot from the scented cotton ball. I didn't know what to do for a while because he was quartering toward me with nothing vital exposed. I would have to go down through the shoulder, and I was getting worried, because if anything can go wrong . . .

Two weeks previous, in the same tree, a doe had moved right underneath my stand and fed on out into the cornfield. A nice buck, probably would have scored 115, followed her trail in. I had him dead to rights, with the same wind arrangement and everything. But all of a sudden the buck just turned and took out of there. I can't believe he winded me.

All I can figure is that there was some other disturbance or scent in the area. I had had other hunters disturbing me and this particular tree. One guy had followed me into the area and wanted to hunt from my stand. He could have been in there in the morning.

So I could see this happening again. The buck stood there and stood there. I decided if he took another step and put his antlers down, I'd shoot. He did. I shot between the antlers and skated the arrow in where it belonged.

Everything turned out fine, but it was a matter of keeping cool, not forcing anything, letting the situation develop, knowing what to do and when, moving slowly and having everything on me, the bow and the stand absolutely quiet. Remember, there was no air movement except for a very light breeze.

Weather

A) Storm front moving in. Deer are going to move and move earlier. They'll feed actively.

I've also noticed in our area that after a big snowfall there is very *little* deer movement, contrary to accepted behavior. It's like every deer in the woods disappears. Maybe they ate so much before the storm that they're still digesting it and aren't hungry. I don't know. But give them another day and they're fully active again.

B) Wind. Wind doesn't bother me at all, because it doesn't bother deer unless it is practically a howler. Then no one wants to be anywhere but in some protected area, including me.

What really spooks me are the extremely calm days. There's no denying its beautiful in the woods then, but the hunting can be terrible. The deer can pick up every little sound. Movement in trees will stand out more, too, because they will be isolated instances and more likely to draw attention.

I'd rather hunt on a windy day; I can get away with more in movement and sound. Winds will overpower thermal effects, so I don't need to worry about thermals.

Deer probably will restrict their movement more to the woods, but that's alright because it is where we will be set up.

Constant winds are obviously best; you can figure where your scent will go, and brush movements will be constant so an unusual movement — such as a deer's leg stepping forward or the backline showing up — will still be fairly noticeable. You simply have some predictability.

Swirling winds are bad news, hard to hunt. If you don't see anything on such days, it is not because deer are nervous and can't hear well, it's because they caught your scent. They don't need to smell you a lot to know you're there, so one whiff usually is plenty.

If you're sitting in a relatively small patch of woods, or watching an area that has only one or two approach directions for deer, swirling winds will stop everything for you.

But if you have an area where animals move through from several directions, then you have a chance. Sure, you'll spook some, but some will get through without winding you and possibly offer a shot.

If there's swirling wind, I like to get as high as possible in the tree or on the ridge or hill side. There's a better chance winds will be more constant up higher. At the least, maybe my scent will be dispersed more before it gets to areas where it could alarm deer.

On a quiet day, I'd want to get higher on the stand, too. The longer you sit in an area, the more of a scent pool you'll create, spreading in all directions on a calm day . . . another reason I don't like calm days.

Movement and Sound

You can get by with a fair amount of movement if you do it right, even with the animal looking at you. Mostly, this means slowly and smoothly. **Quick moves are easy to see and startling, also threatening.**

From my experience, deer usually spook from a *sound* associated with slow movement than from the movement itself. Unless they are soft, clothes make a slight sound as you lift your arms or draw or twist. Those sounds probably registered with the deer before the movement did, because the sounds would have been less natural than a slight movement in a tree. The sound wouldn't have been of brush rustling or squirrel claws on bark or bird wings beating.

This has a relationship to the old "jumping the string" situation. It's going to happen now and then, but I can't believe it happens nearly as frequently as is reported. I think the animal already is moving defensively before the arrow is on its way. Either the animal heard something or saw an alarming movement or else it is the animal's sixth sense telling it it just about got caught with its pants down.

Nine times out of ten, there's a lot of self-imposed tension on the hunter. There's simply too much he can do wrong, even just a little bit, to make it look like the animal jumped the string.

Sixth Sense

One morning I was sitting in a tree stand and got to thinking. The night before I had hunted a treestand about 200 yards over. A good buck had come up to the scrape line and went up a draw and out of sight. I hadn't scouted the area as well as I should have, and I had misjudged the situation a bit. The buck had been in view the night before but out of range.

I had picked out that first tree stand because I was trying to cover more trails than I should have. I was in this second one 60 yards over and farther up the slope now because it had seemed like the best area to catch that buck coming back down off the ridgetop.

The more I thought about it, however, the more I wondered about this second stand. I could see that the buck would have to come down one of two draws. He could come through either draw, but it seemed that the one which lead to the scrape at the bottom of the slope would be best. So, an hour and a half after daylight, I got out of this stand and repositioned it further up the slope, so I could cover that draw and trails crossing it.

About 20 minutes later, here he came, down the draw I'd figured. The buck was completing a big circle, going up one draw in the evening to a cornfield, probably to check does more than to feed, then spending the night on the ridgetop and coming back down in the morning to check the scrape line. This was all in the same general area, so he wasn't moving that far.

The third draw was the one that could have messed things up, but I decided where I thought the hub of the activity should be, and that's where it was. The night before, I'd been on a good trail, but it was too far from the hub.

The buck came right past my tree, about 15 yards out. I got a good hit and in about 10 yards his hind feed started catching up with his front feet and getting tangled. He fell in plain sight, so I climbed down and field dressed him.

I had seen that buck coming for 100 yards. When that happens, and when the buck comes from where you figured it should, that alone is a kick. There's tremendous satisfaction in knowing that you have figured it right. You still have to put the meat on the table, but at least you've got the right start.

I've changed my mind in the morning when I'm walking out to a stand, just stood there a while and finally went to another stand. I don't know if it was wind conditions or training or what, but **it works and it can work for anyone who works hard enough at developing it.** Some guys will always seem to have it developed better than others, and I think for some it may be more instinctive. That's a statement, not a ready excuse for not doing the homework.

There's no saying that I might not have had the same good results had I gone on into my first treestand choice, but I have faith in what I do. When you make a change, and it works, that's hard to argue with.

The deer has those same instincts but a lot better developed. You can let them come in too close, and they all of sudden appear to sense that

they've been caught with their pants down. I believe there are vibrations or something. After all, we are hunters, and hunters and predators are the same thing.

I've had them in situations where I let them get too close, then they just seemed to casually change their mind, turn and begin heading out. So I actually shot them as they were exiting. In a situation like that, you have to be prepared and know when and how to move and when to shoot. You have to react quickly and smoothly, because often you will get a shot. But that shot opportunity — and there will be only one — will present itself quickly and be gone quickly. The conditions will be good, but they won't be long.

Some deer will really spook, and that leaves nothing for you. A lot of them, however, just seem to begin leaving the area without seeming to leave. There's an "I don't think I want to be here any more, and if I do it slowly maybe no one will notice" atmosphere about it. The deer veers or turns and basically just walks. Sometimes you can't really tell that the deer is about to make things impossible for you, but suddenly there's brush between him and you and then the big devil is gone.

Effects of Spooking a Deer

I might sound like I'm contradicting myself a bit, but I would say that **deer relate to pressure situations in a bit of a positive way, if you work it right.**

They'll run away from the smell or sound or sight or whatever spooked them. They also know when a person leaves the area. So if they were close enough to get your smell, they also know whether you travelled through and left that area.

They tend to run until they're out of sight, then stop and either survey the back trail from there or start circling. The whitetail is curious, it's just that with pressure it controls its curiosity until it gets the hell out of the area where it was spooked.

So if I'm in a tree and a person walks through, there's no reason to be bothered. The other person spooked the deer, not me. Since the deer probably will circle around to check things out, it could just as well sneak right in to me without ever seeing me because its attention would be on something else. I've had this happen.

However, if **you** spook the deer while you are on stand or are going to your stand and are close to it when you spook the deer, go to another stand. This one is goofed up for a while. It needs to get fresh again.

Distance judging

It takes training. But if you've set up the place right, you ought to be able to get 20 yard shots. There's no appreciable difference in visible trajectory at 15 yards or 25 yards, so you ought to be able to line it up and release. The rest should take care of itself.

Same goes for unconventional shot positions. If you set up right, you shouldn't get many of them. And if you practice enough, then you'll be able to handle them when they come.

The thing is — you're supposed to be the one in control. If you're continually having to scramble, being surprised, having deer do "the unexpected," then you haven't prepared right. This will happen, but it shouldn't happen often.

Taking a second shot

If you missed the first one, of course and obviously take it if you can. If you hit the first one, and you get a second one at the same animal, take it. Four holes in that deer ought to be better than two, and you ought to be working for full penetration every time.

I've had a couple of instances where I shot a deer, the deer took off but circled because it didn't know where I was and ran right past me so I shot it again. I have a responsibility to that animal to put it down as fast as possible.

Hunt With a Partner

I hunt by myself a fair amount of time, but I try to hunt with another person as much as possible and practical. Two knowledgeable heads are better than one. You can check more terrain, report your findings to each other, compare notes and often establish patterns more quickly than if you were doing it on your own.

Safety is another good reason. If something does happen, you each know where the other will be. I also leave a note at home so my family will know where I am, should it appear that I've had trouble or should they need to contact me.

The flip side of hunting with others, or course, is that you'd better be good friends and trust each other. You have worked hard to find the good hunting and stand locations, you've spent time and money doing all the work. Sure, it's nice to be generous to a guy and say "Come on out to my area some night."

If you're successful, especially with good bucks, be prepared for criticism and some less-than-friendly response from previous friends. This is another good reason to know your hunting partner(s) well. Jealousy shouldn't creep in.

Being generous doesn't work. Too often, one person invites another, who invites another, and suddenly its Grand Central Station. I've seen this happen too often, so I believe I have a right to be a bit selfish in this regard. You do, too, with your stands.

A cousin of mine wanted to hunt a good farm not too far from our hometown. I used to hunt it but quit because there are too many hunters in the area for my taste. So I took my cousin around one day and found the scrape line that runs down an old logging road through the hills. It still looked good.

I cleared out a treestand for him. It looked so good that I said, "Cousin, I may come out here once a year myself, but I'll let you know that time. You can have it to yourself all the rest of the time."

Unfortunately, he took his buddy out there the next weekend and the guy shot an eight-pointer off that stand.

I said, "Cousin, you're never going to have that spot again. Kiss it good-bye."

He did, and he hasn't had that stand since. But that stand sees plenty of hunter use.

• Hunting with a partner is especially enjoyable when the results are like this. Morrison and Fratzke took these Wisconsin bucks on November 12, 1982. Morrison's eight-pointer dressed 167 pounds; Fratzke's 10-pointer dressed 189. Both were taken between 4 p.m. and 4:10 p.m.

• Top, a treestand carried on your back leaves one hand free to ward off brush, carry a flashlight, drag a buck, etc. Below, in cold weather, dress to be comfortable. You'll hunt better.

Hunting

• *Fratzke demonstrates another scent-marking technique bucks use. They chew a twig above a scrape, then rub the twig in their pre-orbital gland.*

Hunting

• Sometimes it all goes according to plan (Fratzke's buck scored 146-4/8), sometimes the only thing you'll see is squirrels. A little shooting practice never hurts. You'll notice, too, that squirrels often are a much larger target than a deer. Or else it just seems that way.

Chapter 5
Late Season Hunting

The deer — does, yearlings and bucks — usually are bunched up; they're more visible; they usually have to travel further to find feed; they tend to travel later in the morning and earlier in the evening.

In the late season, most of us have used up our vacation time, so we have only a limited amount of hunting time. (This is another good reason for thorough scouting from year to year.) Most of our hunting time now will be on weekends. Even though the pressure will be light, we still need to be able to make best use of the time available.

Several years ago, when I was just about the only bowhunter in the areas I hunted, I would have good shooting until 9 a.m. or 10 a.m. As hunting pressure increased, good shooting at that time of the morning became rare. Good shooting moved up a couple of hours, closer to daylight, because the deer adjusted.

One, two or even three bucks may be chasing the same unbred does. Since the deer will be fairly well bunched up, it stands to reason that

• In late season, bucks will show at the marked points, as they will during early season. However, now, especially during the late rut, they're just as likely to cross right through the open. They tend to take the shortest route between food and cover now.

• *A pine plantation has all sorts of cover during a snowstorm. Deer were moving when this snowfall began, but all that came of it was a nice walk in the woods during some interesting weather.*

Late Season Hunting

there will be more competition for the unbred does. This helps your odds.

Those bucks also will make scrapes, just as they did in November. Scrapes in the primary — and many secondary — areas are good to hunt now, just as before.

In this weather and general climate, even if a wind is bad, deer will still take the shortest route, which sometimes leaves them exposed. I think it has to do with energy conservation and the fact that with less hunting pressure they relax a bit.

This relaxation factor is important in morning hunting, as noted earlier. And, of course, in late season it usually is easier to get between them and their bedding area (compared to early season) because generally they're moving farther. This lets the area around your stand cool down after you get into it and before they show up.

Where I hunt, there are plenty of ridges and valleys. For a whitetail hunter in flatter country, feed sources (except for oak ridges — when there are acorns and when the snow isn't too deep) will still be mostly out in the open. Deer are going to take advantage of cover more than in my area. There will be more cover on the shortest routes between feeding areas and bedding areas, but they still will be concentrated in protected low spots or conifer thickets.

We had a bad winter in the ridge country a few years ago that I wish I had photographed. All the deer bedded under big pine trees where the boughs were covered with snow and drooped to the ground. It was like cities under there. You couldn't believe the deer pellets. They lived there; it was terrific cover.

This was up on top near a point of land. All the deer had to do to see for miles was to stick their heads out from under the pines. The snow wasn't quite as deep up on top of the ridges, and they were close to the cornfields.

This wasn't anything new for the bucks, though. They generally bed high, near the break in the ridge or on the side of a point. They can be almost impossible to get at or even see. **With the wind at their back, they can smell what's behind them on the ridgetop, they can see what's in front of them on the side of the ridge below them as well as up and down the slope near them, and their ears can pick sounds up everywhere.** If they're spooked, in two jumps in any direction they have a lot of ridge and timber between them and whatever spooked them.

On warm winter days, you're going to see more deer activity. Does and fawns will come out earlier in the afternoon all the time, but much earlier on these days. Warm, sunny winter days make us feel good; there's no reason to believe the deer wouldn't be affected the same.

When I'm setting up close to bedding areas, I have to remember that **sound travels further in late season.** Seems like it travels twice as far.

• These two bucks were taken December 16, 1978. Len Anglewitz, left, took his 152-2/8 Pope and Young score buck in late afternoon; Bob Fratzke took his 157-2/8 score buck around 7:30 a.m. These bucks were taken during the rut.

There's less foliage to absorb sound and the air is clearer. This means I have to be careful setting up the stand close to a bedding area. It's a judgment thing — clearness of the day, wind or no wind, etc.

Scent is always a consideration, as a factor of wind direction, but from my experience we usually remember that and forget the problem of sound carrying. Other wildlife isn't as active, either, and surrounding sounds, such as kids shouting or farm tractors working, aren't as frequent. So there's more silence, which means any of your clothing or equipment noises will be more noticeable and will carry further. You think an arrow drawn across an unsilenced arrow rest can sound like a violin in November? Try it in December. It will sound like a whole orchestra, and all out of tune.

Dress right, think right

Late season hunting is tougher. Winds cut like a knife. It can get so cold you turn blue. You wonder whether your back and arm muscles might pop if you try to draw. You never know if the wind chill will be 10 above or 20 below. So you have to pay attention to the details and be prepared.

You have to have the right clothes and then dress right so you can sit for a few hours. It takes a special dedication in this manner just to buy the extra clothes and equipment. A lot of hunters have a pair of camouflage pants and a suit of insulated underwear and think they're set for the whole season.

It takes a lot more. You have to have good gloves or mitts. A mitt with a slotted palm is excellent. Mitts are warmer than gloves, simply because it is easier to warm a whole hand in a pocket than single fingers in stalls. You also can move your hand, wiggle your fingers, clench your fist inside a mitt without creating noticeable movement.

You have to be warm and comfortable. If you aren't, your confidence and concentration leave there for someplace warm. There are times you want to get out of the stand and run, not walk, back to the truck.

I have a tough time with my feet. They get so cold I sometimes wonder if it's worth it. (It is.) Scent doesn't carry as much on the cold, dry air of winter, but I still wear insulated rubber boots.

The rest of my outfit is keyed around layers of medium-weight items so there's plenty of trapped air. My knitted acrylic sweaters are good, but in coldest weather, I'll go to the heavy acrylic or knitted wool. Under it, I'll have insulated underwear and wool shirts. A light nylon windbreaker under this stuff helps cut the wind, if the wind is a problem. The only thing you want to be sure of here is that you aren't overheated when you put the windbreaker on. It can trap moisture given off by your body and that can chill you quickly.

Layered clothing can be carried to your stand, so you're not overdressed while walking in. This keeps your body from overheating. Then

• *This strip of pines looks exposed and is exposed. However, during the rut deer come straight over the top of the ridge (from direction of camera) and through it, and they also run right along it. That's why the bowhunter has a comfortable, barely noticeable stand in one of those pines.*

you can put on extra clothes as you cool down. You'll cool down fast, so it's not as if you were to stand in the woods and spook everything by adding another item every ten minutes.

If you keep your kidneys warm and your neck warm, that goes a long way. In super cold weather I'll wear a ski mask that leaves only my eyes uncovered.

An insulated pocket hung on your belt will do most to keep your bow-hand warm. This pocket can carry a few essential accessories, too, if needed. The only concern I have about this item, and it is a minor concern, is that you have to move your hand a couple of feet to get on the bowstring. But if you know when and how to move, this shouldn't be a big concern. If it is, stick your hand in your vest or jacket pocket, which will have it closer to the right position on the bowstring.

I like vests for inner wear in cold weather. They keep my body warm without adding bulk on my arms. The last thing I want is something getting in the way of the bowstring as I draw or as I release.

Treestands in winter

Don't be afraid of setting up a treestand for late season hunting. If you can't set up in a protective pine or other conifer tree, you might worry about possibly being skylined or sticking out like a sore thumb. You don't need to worry if you prepare right.

Don't wear camouflage clothing that is very dark. Wear browns and tans, or some of the winter-designed patterns. Be sure the camo pattern has big spots; smaller lines and spots tend to run together from a distance. Since the woods is more open this time of year, you want to be part of that overall appearance. A camo outfit that is too dark seems to exaggerate your presence in the tree.

I don't put different camo on my bow for winter, because I usually have it camouflaged in fairly light tones all during the year. The bow will be hanging on a peg or branch stub, so its thin lines blend well with whatever brush or branch background exists.

The bulk of your body now is the big concern, which is a bit of a switch from the early season.

• A late season stand with attached camo bag, including suspenders, is a comfortable combination. Sure keeps the wind off you. When the moment comes, you're warm and ready. The bag has enough length to allow easy swiveling to shoot in either direction or behind the tree. In the other photo, Bob, boy (son Mark) and a keeper buck.

Late Season Hunting

Chapter 6
Treestands, Camouflage, Scents and Such

Treestands

Treestand? It isn't too big. It has to be simple. It has to be quiet to put up. That's probably one of the biggest things . . . **quietness when putting it in place.**

I hunt with three types of treestands. Each has its own purpose, based on how long I'm going to stand and how far I have to go to get to the stand.

I have two types I can pack on my back, a light version and a heavy version. The light one is 17 inches by 22 inches. It weighs 10 pounds. I don't like to hunt with it that much because the boards are a bit on the thin side, but when I have to walk in a couple of miles, the lightness is great. It has no seat.

• The twig you never saw is the one which grabs the arrow. So remove it. With two guys, it's much easier . . . one on stand directing and one trimming. Trail crosses photo in the foreground. A padded reel bag keeps tree steps from rattling.

Treestands/Camo/Cleanliness

• *Carpeting on your stand will make it quieter and more comfortable. Just be sure you don't get ice on the carpeting. It will be noisy, slippery and less comfortable.*

The heavier backpack model is 16 inches by 24 inches and weighs 15 pounds. I'll use it when I don't have to walk so far. The boards are thicker and stronger. Besides, it doesn't take much to add five pounds to a tree-stand, and carrying those added five pounds far isn't much fun.

The third one is for when I'm going to be on stand all day. It has a seat. This "hotel" model is 19" x 29". I haven't found too many models that have a good, comfortable seat which also can be moved back out of the way when I want to stand. A seat ought to be padded a bit — or a lot. Modify a stand with just canvas and frame seat, because the front part of the frame will cut off circulation to your legs and they'll go to sleep. Cover the front frame with pipe insulation rubber, and you will sit more comfortably.

You want the seat to move out of the way when you stand up so you have enough room to stand comfortably and lean against the tree. You'll also need this space if you have to take a shot around the back side of the tree.

Shapes, configurations and the direction the trunk leans are also important factors. Some tree stands fit better in some trees. Basically, you put stands in only two types of trees — one which has a completely vertical trunk or one which has a trunk leaning back slightly away from the prime area you're covering. It's impossible to stand comfortably in any tree which leans forward, so forget about that type.

I prefer a rope attachment over chain, mainly because of the noise factor. Rope also is a lot warmer in the hands on cold mornings.

Why Take Your Stand Out?

I almost always take my portable stand out with me when I climb down in the evening and then put it back up in the morning.

One reason is that I don't always know where I'm going to stand the next morning, but I **do** know it won't be where I was the night before. Another reason is that I don't want snow or ice buildup on the carpet of my stand.

So much depends on wind direction. Sometimes, it **all** depends on wind direction. The wind changes a lot, even in the winter. When I get to an area I want to hunt, I'll pick my stand site by whatever the wind tells me will be best.

The stand has to be quiet at all times. That's why I use one I can tie in. I don't want it shifting or flexing. Every one of my stands has carpeting on the platform. This is more comfortable to stand on, and it is quiet.

Get moisture on that carpet, however, and you can lose it all. The platform will be slippery, noisy and uncomfortable.

To keep moisture off the stand, be sure you knock the snow from your boots before you step onto the carpeting. Snow melts under pressure, then freezes. So you don't want to stand on any snow, not even have it stuck to the soles of your boots.

A third reason I carry the stand in and out with me is that **I don't like to advertise where I hunt.** Every time you leave a tree stand up, you're leaving an invitation to any hunter wandering through to climb up, take a look, decide he likes it and stay. I have enough trouble finding good stand locations; I don't want to give them away.

• *A boat cleat holds the tie rope securely in Fratzke's mummy bag stand.*

Treestands/Camo/Cleanliness

• *For long waits, a solid stand with a comfortable seat is hard to beat. The best seats can be pushed back when you stand. Stand as much as you can, for this is easier shooting than when you're seated. A clump of trees like this makes a good stand location if everything else is right. You will be well covered.*

Treestands/Camo/Cleanliness   97

Camouflage

The hat has to have some kind of brim, and the entire thing, hat and brim, must be soft. If it had a hard brim, you couldn't draw the bowstring into it. The brim should be large enough to shade the sun but small enough that it won't block part of your vision when the bowstring presses against it.

I use either a face mask or camo cream, depending upon how cold it is. I usually use black cream; it has the best camo effect. Browns and greens don't have that much camo effect, although a combination of black and green is good to get the right light/dark contrast you want.

The face mask, tucked under your collar, keeps the wind off your neck. Zip up your sweater around it and you'll have an important warming factor. **Keeping warm is an important part of total camouflage.**

Jackets, shirts, sweaters and pants ought to have big, bold patterns for most effectiveness. Camouflage patterns that have too-small dots or lines or whatever tend to blend together and make you appear as a solid object.

The key to effective camo is degree of contrast between light tones and dark tones. This is why black is so important; it gives you the dark extreme. Contrasted with light tan or light green or gray, you get the right effect. Two tones of green are about as poor a camo pattern as there is. There just isn't enough contrast.

To evaluate any camo best, look at it in poor light. After all, you will position yourself in the woods so you will be best hidden, and that means out of direct sunlight, back in the shadows or partial shadows. Color intensity is much less in poor light, which is why light/dark tonal contrast is more important than the actual color. Recent research has shown that deer can see some color but apparently not as good as us, with their color pickup best in direct light and poorest in low light. We're all that way, so if we just use common sense we can see why the contrast is important.

There are a lot more light-tone items in the woods than most people realize. Look at the undersides of leaves on a windy day; sometimes they almost twinkle. Look at the light green leaves and shiny grass. For these reasons, I like something close to a 50-50 balance between light and dark tones, maybe a little above 50 percent on the dark tones.

My overall favorite is brown-phase camo, with black, medium brown and light tan coloration. That will work in practically any cover anywhere. Naturally, if you're hunting in prairie country or somewhere else the vegetation is close to a solid background, you might want to consider some variations on this so you will have closer to a solid pattern broken with plenty of thin lines of varying contrast.

Yellow can be a good camo color, as the light part of the tonal contrast. Take a look at a quaking aspen area out west sometime and all you'll see is yellow and other light tones, except for the shadows. There, yellow and black would give you good contrast and also take care of whatever color

• *Good light/dark tonal contrast makes effective camouflage. Note that green camo, right, has less tonal contrast and this is easier to see.*

considerations you would be concerned with.

When you're hunting in snow, you have to adapt to that background in general and your immediate background in particular. Some areas you might want almost all white, but most areas you'll want white or gray and dark brown or black. If you're on the ground, you probably would want more white or gray than dark tones; in a tree, the condition might be reversed. You wouldn't want to look like a big, white moth clinging to the side of a tree.

Wear a camouflage tee-shirt, because when you're hunting you can't have your outer garment buttoned or zipped tight all the time or you would overheat. A solid-tone tee-shirt would make too large a block.

Hands . . cover with gloves or camo cream. I wear gloves from the start of season to the end because I don't like to have to put the camo grease on and then wash it off every time. In addition, by the time you get to your stand it is gone, either sweated or unintentionally rubbed off. (Same for the face; you can sweat off camo grease in warm weather.)

All this camo pattern information is no good unless you **apply it to clothing that is soft and silent.** Soft and silent means in the woods, not rubbing it between your thumb and forefinger at the store counter. This is just as important, if not more important, than the camo pattern, because when the deer is in shooting range silence in movement usually counts more than anything else.

You can soften camo by washing it a couple of times, but then you must be careful that it doesn't fade. **Faded camo is no camo.** In fact, with faded camo you stand out like a sore thumb.

• *Faded camo is no camo.*

I've mentioned that I wear rubber boots all the time. Where I hunt, and for my type of hunting, that's fine. However, I wouldn't recommend rubber boots everywhere, especially where you have to do a lot of walking. In the West, good leather boots are best for general walking, and tennis shoes or running shoes are excellent for final stalking. So are stocking feet. A lot of guys take off their boots and put on a thick pair of socks over their other socks for final stalks. If you use tennis shoes or running shoes, they ought to be dark. There are good camo shoes coming onto the market.

Remember, too, that **there are other types of camouflage just as important as the clothes you're wearing.**

Silence is camouflage, as I noted earlier. Having the knowledge to get in the right position so the animal approaches to good shooting range and doesn't know you're anywhere around — that's effective camouflage. Knowing when and how to move, and when and how **not** to move — that's effective camouflage. Confidence, which lets you sit quietly without fidgeting or thinking you ought to be someplace else . . . comfort on stand . . . using the wind right . . . keeping your body and clothes clean . . . using binoculars and rangefinders to check things without walking to them . . . insect repellents . . lure scents used properly . . . rubber boots which won't pick up foreign scent or disperse your own foot odors . . . getting higher in the tree . . . clearing your stand so you won't brush against twigs . . . those are all effective camouflage techniques as well as just plain good hunting techniques.

Another thing regarding treestands — be sure you have the *bottom* of it camouflaged and you have broken the general outline of the stand platform.

Conifer trees generally make excellent stand sites. You can clear out a couple of branches and get back next to the trunk. The branches sweep out nicely and sort of cradle you back against the trunk. Any animal moving past from almost any direction will have a tough time seeing you, and the branches provide almost a solid background.

Camouflage extends to your bow, accessories and personal ornaments. The bow, with your hands and face, move more than anything else, so common sense tells you they all should be camouflaged. At the very least, camouflage bow and hands. Buttons and buckles and zippers and watchbands and rings and eyeglasses can twinkle. Cover what you can, remove what you can, camouflage the remainder. With glasses, stand in the shade and/or have the sun at your back. Maybe paint the frames dark, if they aren't already dark. Some hunters apply adhesive tape to the frames to cut glare, then use black magic marker to cover the tape.

A large padded pocket hanging from your belt is a must for cold weather hunting, as far as I'm concerned. Keeps your bowhand warm, and it also can hold a lot of accessories. I often put my buck lure in there so it is handy when I need it.

I don't like to use a handwarmer because most types that I've found emit an odor that is totally out of place on a deer stand.

If you're worried about keeping your kidneys warm in cold weather, wear layered clothing and be sure the clothes are long enough to cover your lower back at all times, even when you raise your arms to draw.

• *Left, green camo must have very dark and very light greens, as this does, to be effective. Many greens don't have enough contrast. Above, a hat must shade the eyes but not interfere with the bowstring.*

Cleanliness and Scents

I shower immediately before going out each time, if at all possible. If not, I wash thoroughly. I use unscented soap, Phisoderm and baking soda. I wear clean clothes each time. I wear rubber boots exclusively because they shed scent, and I wear my pants cuffs inside the boots to help hold in my own scent and whatever foot odor I have. Foot odor can be controlled with baking soda, drying of feet and boots, and with good care. Just another detail that's important and cannot be overlooked.

What happens to most hunters? Their time allotted for hunting generally is after work on weekdays or on weekends. After work, during the first part of the hunting season, most states are still on daylight saving time, so that gives you an extra hour to hunt.

Most guys climb into their hunting clothes and go. That's not good.

Be sure the clothes are clean — washed in a non-scented detergent in cold water is best. Maybe put some pine or other appropriate-to-your-area scent in the rinse cycle. Keep them in a bag someplace where they won't absorb cooking odors at home, or even just the general smell of the house. That odor is foreign to the woods.

Wash or shower before you leave home or camp. Don't wear your hunting clothes when you're driving to the hunt site.

Don't smoke in the car, and don't smoke in the woods. Smoke clings to clothes and hair something awful.

If you feel like stopping at a bar after the hunt for a quick pop, change out of your hunting clothes. I always carry an extra pair of jeans, another shirt and a non-hunting type of jacket. This keeps my hunting clothes clean. It also does something else — it helps the hunter's general image. We always hear so much about hunters being drinkers. Some are, some aren't. Either way, it does no good to have a bunch of guys standing around a bar in hunting clothes. Bad for the image and bad for the hunting. If you think you can smell bad all on your own, take a good whiff of yourself and your clothes sometime after you've been in a bar.

The only scent I ever use is buck sex lure during the rut. I don't believe you need anything else, and you don't actually *need* any scent. Good scouting and good hunting technique, applied properly, will do a good job for you.

Bowhunters are so faddish that they jump onto the hot item or idea without taking the time to think it through. It's easier to take a shortcut. But shortcuts can't take the place of sound basics. Every athletic team knows that sound fundamentals make winning teams. It's the same way with hunting.

If you wash, keep your clothes clean, pay attention to the wind and get in a good position, you'll be alright. That's the combination which has worked for me for a long time.

• Left, leaves camouflage the bottom of a treestand well; clumps of leaves are nothing unusual in the woods. Lower left, rubber boots will shed scent and contain food odors. Wear your pants cuff inside the boot to contain odors even more and retain heat in cold weather. Lower right, hang a sex lure scent bottle or can about 18 inches off the ground so thermals or other light breezes can move the scent. Remove the scent when you leave. Use a new container and fresh scent each time, and use it lightly.

• *Son Erik is still working on his first big buck, but you can tell he was pleased to pose with Bob and Bob's buck. Erik shouldn't have any trouble knowing what to look for.*

• *Even when you have permission and even when it's cold, it doesn't hurt to stop and say hello.*

Chapter 7
Landowner Permission — the Key to Good Hunting

There never will be too much emphasis on this topic, for without private land to hunt on we don't have anything. Public hunting land certainly wouldn't meet sport hunting's and sport hunters' needs alone.

Too many hunters (one is too many, actually) resist asking permission of landowners to hunt their land, as if they had some right to trespass. They either drag their feet and do it at the last minute (which is a big mistake) or don't ask at all and either brazenly trespass or sneak on (bigger mistakes).

I don't see how anyone can hunt under those conditions. For one thing, you have to put yourself in sort of a combative frame of mind to do it, and that's no way to spend the day. You're not putting anything over on anyone. From a purely selfish standpoint, it is stupid not to get trespass and hunting permission because without it you can't even hunt properly even if you would sneak on. You couldn't scout it right, and all you would be doing is goofing up whoever had permission to be there.

Have respect of the landowner, his/her land and his/her problems — only so much land, possibility of too many people wanting permission to hunt, previous bad experiences, crops are money, etc. **Show your respect** of the landowner and his/her situation.

Start early. Five minutes before season opens is not the time to win friends and favorably influence people, nor are you likely to find any land not already spoken for.

I start right with late season scouting. I ask permission from the landowner to go on his land to scout. I tell him I've looked at it on maps and from the air and that it looks interesting. I tell him that if subsequent checking shows as much potential as early checking, I'd want to bowhunt for deer on his land next season. I explain that I will be buck hunting. (This is explained because some people are opposed to having does shot. Shoot a doe on such a person's property and you might not get on there again.)

The fact that I've devoted that much effort to scouting almost always interests the landowner. When I show him photos from my flyover, he usually becomes even more interested. Not that many of us have seen aerial photographs of our home turf, so naturally that's going to be interesting.

If things work out well, I'll often give the landowner an enlarged color print of the best aerial photo of his buildings and nearby surrounding land.

I tell the landowner that I will inform him every time I plan to be on his land — even when just scouting — and where I plan to be. If he objects to some or all of my plans, we can work out a solution with friendly discussion.

Once I have permission or as extra inducement to get permission, I give the landowner my business card and home phone number and address, make and description of my car and license plate number. It stands to reason that if you voluntarily give someone all that information, you are serious and aren't planning to goof yourself up. You and he both know he will be checking with you first if something is wrong on his land.

Ask whether the landowner minds if you come at early hours and/or leave at late hours. A barking dog in the morning can wake a family unnecessarily. It is good practice to tell the landowner the approximate hours of the morning or evening you will arrive and depart.

Explain that you open gates and you close them immediately; that you don't drive across new seeding, hay or grain fields, nor do you even turn your vehicle around in them. Add that you stay on their roads and machinery paths, and that you even stay off them when conditions are muddy. (They'll let you know if it is ok to drive on muddy paths on the back 40.) You will be willing to park in the yard or anywhere else they want you to park. Some will want you to park in the yard, others say it is allright to drive closer to your hunting spot if you wish. I prefer leaving the vehicle in the yard or out of sight if I park closer to the hunting spot. This does less to advertise my presence to deer and to other hunters.

Don't dress or act like a slob. Dress decent and normally, not in your hunting clothes, when you ask permission. Wear good clothes, not old ragged ones. It's not a bad idea to dress in non-camo clothes for your scouting efforts; I lost some hunting land one time because the landowner didn't like to see me in camo then. "I don't know what you're doing down there," he said, "but if you have to wear that stuff now, it can't be good."

If you have to be wearing your hunting clothes when you ask permission, you're several months or weeks too late to be doing any efficient hunting anyway, so why spoil it for yourself and potentially for other hunters?

Be clean and neat at all times.

It's good to know something about the landowner, the land, crops, market prices, stock and such ... but don't go overboard. That landowner more than likely is going to be quite reserved, sizing you up. There's no sense trying to be too sympatico when you really aren't. Phoniness is transparent and a gigantic turnoff. Babbling on and on about subjects you think the landowner will be interested in usually is just as bad, unless you like the taste of your own shoe leather. Motor-mouthing usually is a sign of nervousness, and the landowner more than likely will wonder what you're so all-fired nervous about.

However, if the landowner wants to talk, by all means talk — even during the season when you drive in and expect to hop out of the truck and get to your stand. Give up some hunting time if need be. Without that person's permission, you have nothing.

It's just plain common sense to get to know the landowner a bit. Easy conversation, most likely in bits and pieces from time to time, is the best way to do it. This builds good relations for you and for other hunters. In addition, if you get along well enough, he'll probably keep his land for you and turn down others. This is extremely important when the landowner wants to limit the number of hunters on his land, and most do. First come, first served ... if you do it right.

If you have a chance during the non-hunting months to provide some physical labor for the landowner, do it if you know what you're doing. Trying to help with farm work when you really don't know what to do is highly entertaining to the landowner at times, but it also can slow down the work or be dangerous. You don't mess around with farm machinery worth several thousand dollars unless you know what you're doing, and somehow or other the unskilled labor opportunities, such as cleaning calf pens in the spring, doesn't occur to many people. If it does occur, it usually is quickly put out of mind.

In most instances, gifts are the most logical way to express your thanks. I've found that leather work gloves are excellent; landowners/farmers always need more gloves. Sometimes I'll bring a frozen venison steak or roast, but I ask first. A smoked fish is almost always accepted. The only time I'll even consider giving booze or beer is when I know in advance the guy will accept it.

I always send Christmas cards. And I stop to talk now and then even if I'm not intending to go on their land at that time. I also talk freqently with guys on whose land I've hunted for years. They've become friends. Sometimes they also give me some good tips about bucks they've seen. If they have kids who seem interested in bowhunting, I help them out now and then. I also drill them on the do's and don'ts of good scouting, on the gentleman's agreement of stand locations and such.

Once you get to know the landowners, and they trust you, they may never question what you do or where you go — but that doesn't mean you can violate that trust.

Good things sort of mushroom. One landowner might turn you on to another. When my family and I go out for dinner, we see these people, who are now our friends, and we talk and have a good time. They talk with each other, too — about people like us.

If you get turned down, accept it. Maybe the landowner already has enough hunters on his land; if this is the case, I wouldn't want to hunt there anyway. If a guy turns you down once, it doesn't have to mean forever. People change their minds.

Not everyone can have enough land to hunt on. Even if you have a lot of land to hunt, it still isn't enough. You won't get more, though, without recognizing who holds the key to the hunting land and doing right by him.

• *Park your vehicle where the landowner asks you to. He'll feel better, you'll feel better, and the vehicle will be less likely to be spotted by other hunters.*

Chapter 8
The Most Common Questions

Good speakers do three things in their speeches: 1) Tell you what they're going to tell you; 2) tell you; 3) tell you what they've told you. That helps the message get through.

So, even though we have talked about most or all of these subjects earlier in the book, here's a run-through of the questions I'm most commonly asked.

1) Can you move at all on the stand?
Definitely. This is the only way you could stay several hours. But you can't jump and twitch and fidget. When I say "moving," first check the area. Turn your head from side to side, checking where you think the animals are going to approach. If you've been in the woods a lot, you can spot animals much faster than someone who hasn't. That's just like going out West for the first time . . . someone who lives and hunts there a lot

can see animals much more quickly than we can. They know what to look for.

That's also where scouting comes in — you get practice at seeing animals.

You pick out ears, a backline, the face of one looking right at you. You'd be surprised — or maybe you wouldn't — over the number of times you spot deer when you're slowly turning your head.

You survey the area, survey it again. Then you move your leg to ease a sore muscle, or stretch to help your back.

That's a good reason to have a seat on a stand, especially if you're going to be a long time. Sitting for a short time gives your legs and feet a rest.

2) What about standing up and sitting down?

Basically, for all shooting, **standing is best.** Sitting down is a hard way to shoot; it seems tougher to come to full draw, and it definitely reduces your flexibility.

For me, standing up helps keep me alert. If I sit down, I'm dozing in five minutes. That can be dangerous, and it misses deer.

3) What do you do with your bow? Can you hang it up without hurting your chances?

Many stands come equipped with brackets to hold your bow. I'd rather hang it in a tree on an overhanging branch within easy reach. Then I can just reach out a little bit, unhook the bow and start coming to full draw. That seems to be mostly a downward movement, which is much less noticeable in the woods than an upward movement.

When I'm scouting and clearing stands, I'll often nail a Y branch horizontally to a main branch, nailing through both tips of the Y. I'll fasten it in a position that will let me turn without the bow, then pick it up and draw. For instance, rather than try to move the bow out around a tree, or through a big crotch, I'll hang the bow on the back side, then lean around or through with my body, pick up the bow and draw. I don't make much movement that can be detected. Seems like **the bow with a quiverful of arrows gets unconsciously waved around a lot,** and that can be easy to see. So — again, the value of good scouting — if you know where the deer are likely to come from, you can have your bow ready and make less movement to get the job done.

Another thing you definitely want are **small pockets on the front of your pant legs,** just above the knee. Rest the lower limb tip in one of them. That takes the weight off your arms and shoulders, but it keeps the bow in almost a ready position.

4) How do you locate bucks?

I think we've covered that.

5) How high should a tree stand be?

I like it 15 feet off the ground, as a rule. I'd rather be a little bit lower than too high. If it's too high, you're starting to have too many overhanging branches in the way. This also causes a bad shot angle, makes your target a lot harder to hit.

6) What type arrow, fletch and broadhead do you use?

Type of broadhead is a personal matter entirely, but it must be sharp, sharp, sharp. If you shoot a broadhead once, replace the blades or, if it is a fixed-blade style, sharpen it again. Too many people are satisfied with a blade that is less than sharp.

I use feather fletching, four fletches, four or five inches long, helical or offset. I'd recommend helical to be safest. Attachment is 75/105 on most, 90 degrees on some. I get good arrow flight with four-fletch, the setup is very forgiving, and I have good results in balancing arrows. Feathers are a bit lighter than vanes, and since you want the broadhead always to be a little heavier than the fletching for best flight, the balancing works well this way. Even if the head is only 120 grains, it still is heavier.

Never put the fletching on straight. You need that arrow rotating to get the best spin stabilization. Fletching makes the spin, not the broadhead blades.

Snap-on nocks are the best all around because they keep the arrow from falling off your string. The only thing I don't like about them is that if you need or get a second shot, sometimes that snap of nock on string carries quite a distance no matter how you try to muffle it. A nock that is too small will really snap, and it will give a poor release and arrow flight.

• *A good quiver will space the arrows well enough that they won't brush against each other and rattle.*

7) When during the season do you usually see and kill your trophy bucks?

During the rut and the late (December) season. They are more active, more visible.

8) Does smoking bother deer in the woods?

I think it does. It's a foreign odor that carries a long distance and has staying power. Smell your clothes some morning after you spent a couple of hours in a bar the night before. They reek.

How much do you want the buck? If you want it enough, you'll keep yourself and your clothes clean, and you'll forget about smoking in the woods.

9) Are there some things you *always* do?

Yeah. I've always scouted an area before I hunt it. I always try to shower before I go into the woods and be sure my clothes are clean. I always wear rubber boots. I always am dressed right so I can stand comfortably and be well camouflaged.

The scouting, particularly, gives last-minute options. Last year, for instance, on opening day I moved into an area that only I had permission to hunt. When I came to my stand, close to where I knew the deer came out, another hunter was set up 30 yards from my stand.

Since I knew where deer were doing most of their traveling, I went to a spot which watched a couple of trails and climbed into a tree that I didn't even have cleared out. I could have killed a buck that night off that stand. It came right in behind me. Never knew I was there.

My knowledge of the land made that happen.

The other guy never saw a thing. The bit that teed me off the most, though, was that he was goofed up before he started. He was trying to sit in a tree crotch, but he had to lean back. Didn't even have a tree stand. He had no way to shoot in the direction deer were coming from. Then he left a good hour before dark. He was on his way out when I saw the buck.

10) Does noise in the distance bother deer?

No. Those are natural sounds; they hear them every day; they're accustomed to them. They seem to know when they're threatened. If the noise is from something coming toward them, then they'll pay attention until they either take off or dismiss it. Gunshots don't bother them, other than maybe getting their attention a bit. The noise is made and then is gone. Bird scaring devices probably startle you more than they startle deer.

11) When you hunt with the bow during a firearm season, do you do anything different?

I'm hunting under the most intense pressure they will have during the year, so I try to set up on their primary escape routes.

Deer do a lot of moving then. I set up near heavy cover, but they seem to be just going through. They want to get the hell out of the whole area, into the really rough terrain and cover.

There will be people moving, deer moving. The running deer are dead. **The sitters, the hiders, they're the ones which will make it through season.** They're the ones with the smarts and the good nerves.

I haven't noticed deer spooking from orange camo, because I know when to move and when not to move. I'm still highly visible to the human eye, but that doesn't automatically translate into a deer-spooking factor.

Besides, often after the first weekend of the firearm season there isn't much hunting pressure. Deer go back to their basic patterns, to a degree. I've killed good bucks chasing does during the middle of the week of the firearms season, bucks and does moving on their own with absolutely no hunting pressure.

Several things affect them — the hunting pressure, whether or not it is during rut, whether they have adequate excellent cover nearby or have to move out of the area temporarily.

12) Does wind affect deer and how?

Deer travel under any situation except a heavy rain or snow storm. I don't believe wind stops their travel at all. **The main effect of wind is that it makes it harder for you to connect with a deer on a quiet day,** so I like strong breezes and wind. Deer don't hear you as quickly. If a guy complains about the wind screwing up his hunting, he hasn't got it figured out yet. Sure, a knock-down, howling wind will restrict movement, but deer will still find places to travel . . . and not even a wind like that will affect every area of deer habitat.

Last year, when I connected on my Wisconsin buck it was probably one of the most miserable days in the woods. The wind was really blowing. Trees looked like they were going to come loose. It was during the rut, and there were more deer moving in the woods that day than any day I was in the woods.

I went on stand at 12:30 p.m., and by 1:30 I saw deer moving. They weren't feeding, just moving. There was a little snow on the ground, and it was blowing some snow. It had rained most of the week.

Swirling winds and gusts probably make deer nervous as hell, but the only reason you don't see deer on that particular night probably is because they picked up your scent, not because they weren't moving. **Your scent is the number one cause of not seeing a deer.** The only reason most hunters don't see deer in the woods is not because the deer aren't there or aren't moving, it's because the deer have smelled them for one reason or another.

Photo by Mark LaBarbera

13) How do you hunt during wet weather?

If it is a downpour, I don't hunt. No sense in it. If it is misty I may put on some raingear, but I'll have good camo over the top of it to help silence it and hide me. I prefer not to wear rain gear, because I usually won't need it if I'm hunting in the right place and the mist is acceptable. A tree trunk can stop a lot of mist. A pine tree can stop a lot more. In fact, you can be in a spruce or pine and stay dry through some heavy rain.

At the knitting mill (Winona Sportswear), we use wool and acrylic. These shed water well, and the acrylic actually dries faster. Wool has a tendency to keep you warm even when it is wet, but it takes a lot longer to dry. Our washer/dryer setup at work dried wool in 20 to 30 minutes on the hot cycle, but it took only 10 minutes on the cool cycle to dry the knitted acrylic. Acrylic will hold a little oil, too, if it is knitted soft enough, and that helps it shed water.

What I'm saying is that a good wool or acrylic outer garment works

better than rain gear under most conditions because it is silent and keeps you just as dry or drier.

There's no reason to change hunting location. Hunt as usual.

This is an excellent time to use a string tracker. Tracking conditions probably will be all right, but they probably won't be ideal. If you haven't put water repellent on your feather fletching, they can pick up some water and not fly as well as they should. And in these conditions you'll put sensible limits on your shot distance and shot conditions.

There's good hunting in many wet, misty conditions. Deer often move like crazy in a warm rain; seems like they're out to get a bath or something. So if you set sensible limits you'll be all right. If the bowhunters in the Pacific Northwest had to wait for dry conditions to hunt, they'd be waiting yet.

14) How do you figure thermals?

It has a lot to do with the day winds, because they can overpower thermals. That gets back to the fact that I'd rather hunt in the wind than a quiet day. There's tremendous local variation in thermals due to cover and terrain. This, again, gets back to the value of scouting. If you don't scout enough, a rule-of-thumb condition can goof you up entirely. Thermals are like water in their flow, and on quiet days they can flow here and there and around and over . . . and just completely goof things up for you. Your scent may not be washed away at all. In my area, for instance, day winds usually take over around 8:30 a.m., and you see most of the deer after that or 9 a.m. Day winds work better for hunters than thermals.

15) Will big bucks ordinarily look for high ground? How does that match with big bucks in the swamps?

Swamp hiding to high ground hiding are basically the same thing. They're going to go to the best vantage point in their territory, a place they can see well from and with the wind at their back, so their nose tells them what's behind them, their eyes tell them what's in front, and their ears check all around. And then they just remain still. You'd be surprised how a good buck can pick a spot in a small area which allows him good vision yet has him hidden.

16) What about backtracking, doubling back?

If a buck is hit hard, it's just exiting and dropping. If you've got a lesser hit, they definitely do double back, criss-cross, do everything possible to lose you.

When my oldest son shot his first deer, he had a low hit. We trailed that deer eight hours, and the deer was just ahead of us all the time. It crossed its trail six or seven times. We weren't able to intercept it when it did. It simply became a matter of time. When we caught up to the deer, one more shot in the boilerworks finished it. That deer hardly had any blood left in it. The hit was high on the brisket . . . never touched the heart, lungs, anything internal. That deer was dead, but it just kept on going.

17) How can you take the glare from glasses?

Keep the sun to your back and stay in the shadows. That's how you're supposed to be positioned most of the time anyway. Anything looking into the sun cannot see well, and when you're back in the shadows the lower light intensity is helping camouflage you.

Wear a soft brimmed hat, preferably with a short brim so it won't bend down and block your vision at full draw. I've developed a floppy acrylic hat I like.

18) Can you anticipate deer movement changes?

Yes, if you've done your homework. It helps even more if you know what the previous year was like. You know where the food sources are. You know that when the alfalfa is gone, they're going to go to something else. You have a good idea when the acorns will drop, so that will help you predict.

Basically, you have to become a bit of a farmer and a bit of a biologist. You have to know when certain crops are harvested. You have to know the foods deer eat, where to find these foods, when they do mostly grazing, when they pick up on browsing and cut back on grazing, where the white oaks (the favorite deer acorn) are, and things like that. You don't just walk into the woods and mysteriously find deer. You more or less go to school. You work at it, and you study. You make mental notes and notebook notes. You see patterns develop. You know enough about the deer's behavior trends and the plant biology to predict with some certainty just what is going to happen.

Individual deer remain unpredictable, of course — especially if they want to live long — but the species has habits and traits. You have to know them and make use of them.

19) Do you notice any changes in sightings when acorns drop?

Yeah. If you don't find the acorns, especially in a year when there's a good white oak acorn crop, you might just as well hunt trophy bucks in your bathroom. Nothing else matters when acorns are good.

20) Do you ever recommend edge hunting?

Yes. I recommend edge hunting if you want to take a deer for the experience, such as for a beginner getting to know what it is like. You probably will have an opportunity to shoot a doe or small buck a lot sooner than if you're back in the brush waiting for a monster.

At the same time, you have to control yourself. You will have more deer sightings, but many of them won't be any good. You'll have chances for more long, poor shots. Know your limitations. And learn from the fact that deer often come out of the woods onto a field just out of bow range. Why? More than likely because some of them know where you are or have a pretty good idea. They could have picked up your scent running the perimeter trail.

It's easy to get excited about seeing a field full of deer, but if they're all out of range you haven't really accomplished anything other than fooling yourself.

• *We all must start somewhere and learn as we go. Bob Fratzke learned to be an excellent whitetail hunter. You can too.*

21) Is it really necessary to wear complete camo?

Yes, just for the sake that if anything can go wrong it will go wrong. **You go to all the scouting work and other work, why screw it up over sheer laziness or carelessness.** It isn't any big job to camouflage yourself completely. It only takes one mistake to spook an animal. Put camo on your face. Camouflage your hands with grease or gloves. Hands move about as much as anything. Cover shiny items on the bow. Be careful about your watchband. It may be covered when your arms are down, but what happens when you raise your arms to draw? Does the sleeve pull back so your watchband can twinkle in the buck's eyes?

It just doesn't make sense to take needless chances. Yes, use full camo.

22) How important are the arrows?

The first time I heard this question, I didn't quite understand it, so I replied, "Well, they're about all you've got to shoot out of a bow."

That got a laugh, but it wasn't what was intended. The guy wanted to know how much to spend. This has become a typical question, and I don't understand why it should be. **A guy goes to the expense of getting an expensive, high quality bow, he scouts thoroughly, then he chintzes on his arrows and broadheads. That doesn't make any sense.** The only things that are going to do the actual work . . . they get cheap on.

You're far better off spending an extra $3 per arrow/broadhead, or whatever the amount may be. You're less likely to ruin a good arrow. You'll have better matched equipment, which means more accuracy. The only thing which guides the shot right is good fletching on a good arrow.

I also find that the person who chintzes on his arrows tends to shoot dull broadheads. Must be some personality factor.

If you have to economize, broadheads and arrows aren't the place to do it.

23) How much of your knowledge translates to any whitetail area?

Basically it would be good for any whitetail area, because the key thing is to know the area. You know basic whitetail behavior, so you put that together with specialized local information and you're in business.

24) What would be the first things you would do or check if you were going into a new area?

Assuming you're also talking about a different type of terrain, the first thing I'd do is find a reliable contact person in the area, someone who could demonstrate to me his whitetail knowledge and terrain knowledge. There are a lot of contacts in archery. We're all brothers. This cuts down on your homework about 90 percent.

Then you check your topographical maps against what he tells you.

You have studied the animal (if it is a different species). You know the preferred local foods, and you ask about patterns. Even the same species will have regional behavior characteristics, maybe caused by differences in hunting pressure, differences in habitat types, differences in weather, differences in food availability. Then you go look.

25) Does the beginning of the rut change from year to year on a time frame?

No. The amount of light available triggers it. Frost doesn't have anything to do with it. However, cooler weather gets them moving more.

I remember one hot fall that was 70 degrees, 75 degrees, during the first week in November. The does weren't even moving during the day. Bucks would bed with the does, and they'd all stay put during the day. There was no reason for them to move, and they'd do most of their breeding at night.

26) Can you overdo the use of scents?

Yes. Most guys figure that if two drops are great, four ought to be twice as good. It doesn't work that way. **Best to be too light than too heavy.** Another mistake some people make is to put a few drops on a cotton ball today, then add a couple more drops the next day, a couple more the third day, etc., just to freshen it up.

I've gotten so I use a fresh cotton ball each time I go out. This cotton is kept in a plastic 35mm film canister. I use only a few drops, and I just hang the can out where I want it, probably around 15-18 inches off the ground.

When I leave, I cap the canister and take it with me. **Scent shouldn't be left in the woods,** I feel. It can ruin an area's effectiveness if it smells too much or if deer come to it but find nothing.

I'm talking here of the use of sex attractant scent.

Another thing . . . never put that stuff on yourself. Why attract attention directly to yourself? You don't get too many good shots when the buck coming in thinks you're the doe he's looking for.

27) Are there some things with whitetails you can always count on?

Nope. A predictable buck is a dead buck. I'm not the first person to say that, and I won't be the last.

I should change that a bit. Yes, you can figure on one thing from whitetails . . . just when you think you have them figured out, they do something which blows your whole theory out the window. All this tells you is that you probably were trying to jump to conclusions and maybe were taking false readings from the sign in the woods or you really weren't seeing what the signs were trying to tell you. You may have wanted something to develop in a particular way, and you could have tried to

• *There's more out there like this one.*

force it that way. When it didn't work, if you're smart, that's when you wised up.

28) How many places do you hunt?

A couple of dozen completely separate geographical areas. I classify two areas more than a mile apart as being geographically separate regarding deer territory. If the cover is heavy you may not need a mile, but then you're going to have more territorial overlapping.

I have two to four stands in each area, simply to take advantage of wind conditions, morning or evening sun location. I need this many areas and stands, because not all areas are good at the same time, and not all stands are good at the same time. And I sure don't want to over-use an area.

29) How long should you hunt an area before you give up on it?

That's a question which answers itself. Most guys do not have enough area to hunt, or they don't develop enough area to hunt, so they hunt the hell out of one little area. Then they give up hunting there because "there ain't no deer there."

The heck there aren't! They've simply over-used the area. **Most of the time it isn't the area which is bad, the deer simply know you're there and where you are.** Just because you don't see them doesn't mean they aren't there. It's your fault, not the area's fault. The deer just move around you.

30) How long can you hunt a spot before it becomes no good?

We always seem to have luck when we go into an area the first time. If you have enough of these areas to move around in, you can almost, for the whole hunting season, hunt fresh every day. I don't mean you must have a stand each day which you've never sat in before; I mean you need enough so you can rotate, switch, play your hunches.

The trouble most people have is that they don't know where they're going to hunt this evening. They haven't scouted enough to know, so they flip a coin or guess or just wander into the woods and see where they end up. When you've done your homework, and prepared enough areas, you don't have this problem. Like I've said, when you do your scouting the hunting takes care of itself.

31) What style of anchoring, aiming, shooting do you use and why?

I used to shoot instinctively, because I did well with it and enjoyed it. I've modified it a little recently, adding a single sight pin. I shoot a couple of times a week and can judge distance fairly well. You have to keep in form no matter how you shoot, but instinctive shooting especially demands that.

I added the single pin last year only for the close-in shots, to make sure I concentrate and put the arrow where it will do the most good. **Very close shots are the toughest in bowhunting;** because of the nearness of the animal and the tension you put on yourself, it is easy to lose concentration. I was catching myself peeking and pulling the arrow away from my face just to get a look at the animal. I was anticipating, taking that animal before I shot it.

32) What are some of the common shooting form errors bowhunters make?

Peeking is number one. It is the result of anticipation and the lack of control of yourself. A poor or non-existent follow through is next. I'd almost class it as related to peeking, because when you don't complete the shot there's some reason for it, and that reason 90 percent of the time is to see what's going to happen.

Then there's the problem of taking too-long shots, not knowing your limits, not knowing what are good percentage shots and what are low.

Right along with that is the inability to judge distance. We don't judge distance as well as we think we do. It takes practice, and even then you can be off quite a bit. On an arrow trajectory, misjudging by a couple of yards can mean the difference between a good hit and a miss or poor hit.

33) What kind of areas do bucks like to make their rubs in?

Popple thickets in my part of the country are preferred. Evergreen trees are next, particularly small pine. From then on, it mostly is softwood saplings and whips.

This can get pretty involved, which we've done earlier in the book.

34) Do you have to cut the metatarsal glands from the deer?

No. They haven't tainted the meat while the animal was alive, so they won't when it is dead. They don't touch meat. Keep your hands/gloves away from them and close below them on the leg hair when you're field dressing and skinning the animal and you'll be all right. If you get the secretions on your hands/gloves, that's when you — not the glands — can taint the meat.

35) Have you done any rattling?

Yes, but I learned later that what I did was wrong. So I've studied more information and practiced it. I'm going to try again. If it works for some hunters, it ought to work for others.

- *Basing the rattling antlers against your thigh and grinding them gives the sound of heft behind the grinding, as if two bucks were leaning into each other.*

36) Have you tried deer calling?

Yes. It worked for me in some areas but not in others. I don't know why. This is another thing I'm checking in more detail. I haven't been able to call in any big bucks yet, only does and yearlings.

37) This seems weird, but do some people actually use used tampons to attract bucks during the rut?

Yes. There are scented (with a perfume deodorant) and unscented types. The unscented types work best because they don't have the foreign perfume odor. We have talked with several female bowhunters who flatly state they see more bucks than anyone if they are in the midst of a menstrual period and hunting during the rut.

38) Do deer remember?

They sure do. Spook a deer at a stand one night, and you won't see it there the next night or any other night in the near future. If it is a big buck, you may never see it there again.

39) What are your techniques on trailing a wounded deer?

First, accept the responsibility of doing all you can to recover that animal. Trailing is work, but it also is fun. After that . . .

1) Try to see where the arrow hit the deer. Use your binoculars if you can. Quite a few bowhunters do, and it really helps. It is extremely easy to mis-identify the hit location in the excitement and tension.

2) Mark (mentally) by a tree, rock or other object the place you last saw the deer before it moved out of sight, then remember this place.

3) Listen. If you hear the deer fall, then silence, you know it is dead. If you heard a stumbling fall, it is still going.

4) Wait half an hour unless you can see the dead deer. Many deer are lost because the hunter was too anxious, moved in on a mortally wounded deer too early and spooked it into wild flight, flight which left an inadequate trail.

5) Look for the arrow and other signs of a hit. When you find this sign, use it to dictate the manner and quickness with which you'll trail the deer. We could write another chapter on this, but if you're reading this book you should have read and learned most of that information already.

One of the major problems in losing hit deer is the over-anxious bit, especially with gut-shot deer. If you hit a deer in the paunch, leave it alone. If it departs in the direction you were going to go, circle way around it. **Do not disturb it.**

On an evening hit, wait until the next morning to trail it. On a morning hit, wait until two hours before dark to take up the trail. The reason for this is that a paunch hit is a fatal hit but slow acting. A paunch hit deer will seldom go more than 50 yards before bedding down. If you kick it out of his bed, you're in trouble. But if you leave it there, you should come back hours later to a dead or almost dead deer.